Praise for
The Fear Paradox

"A delightfully fearless and deeply sensitive examination of that most primal and formative human experience. I'll be thinking about this book for a long time to come."

—Alan Burdick, author of *Why Time Flies: A Mostly Scientific Investigation*

"Frank Faranda is an accomplished student of the mind, and especially of the interplay between fear and imagination. He's not only a great thinker and writer, but also a terrific storyteller, keen observer of humanity, and gentle mentor on how we can do better."

—Douglas Rushkoff, bestselling author and Professor of Media Theory and Digital Economics at CUNY/Queens

"A tour of psychoanalytical thinking around anxiety and how fear drives us, this is an insightful and informative book that challenges us to face our vulnerabilities so that we can be better and wiser."

—Dr. Stephen Joseph, psychologist at the University of Nottingham and author of *Authentic: How to be Yourself and Why It Matters*

The Fear Paradox

The Fear

Paradox

How Our Obsession
with Feeling Secure
Imprisons Our Minds
and Shapes Our Lives

Frank Faranda, PhD

Coral Gables

For permission requests, please contact the publisher at:
Mango Publishing Group
2850 S Douglas Road, 2nd Floor
Coral Gables, FL 33134 USA
info@mango.bz

For special orders, quantity sales, course adoptions and corporate
sales, please email the publisher at sales@mango.bz. For trade and
wholesale sales, please contact Ingram Publisher Services at customer.
service@ingramcontent.com or +1.800.509.4887.

The Fear Paradox: How Our Obsession with Feeling Secure
Imprisons Our Minds and Shapes Our Lives

Library of Congress Cataloging-in-Publication number: 2020933477

ISBNs: (p) 978-1-64250-057-8 (e) 978-1-64250-058-5

BISAC: HIS035000, HISTORY / Study & Teaching

Printed in the United States of America

To my wife and son

Table of Contents

Introduction

Fear as a Threat

"Fear can transform us in ways that
fundamentally alter how we perceive
our world."

—Henry L. Chambers Jr.

One summer, not so long ago, I got a taste of something long forgotten—the joy of riding waves. I'm not talking about tame little crests, I'm talking about waves that slam you into the sand and carry you for twenty yards. This was what I found one afternoon at Marconi Beach on Cape Cod, riding waves with my twelve-year-old son.

I was already familiar with the waves at Marconi. I had spent a summer on Cape Cod when I was in my twenties, and rode those waves many times. In those days, I was much stronger, but even coming back as an older man, the same excitement drew me in. To my surprise, my son ventured into the water with me. He doesn't typically like riding waves, but I think he could see everyone's enjoyment and decided to jump in. People from age ten to sixty were out there having a ball. I wasn't consciously thinking that the joy I was feeling riding those waves was a result of the proximity to danger, but in hindsight, I suppose it was.

For me, with my son, I was in heaven. We had each ridden about six waves when, all of a sudden, we looked out toward the horizon and saw a huge swell emerging. Along with this swell came a powerful undertow that made it difficult to move. I looked over at my son, and he was preparing to ride. I dove into the wave as it came crashing in on me, and I rode it to the shore. It was big and it threw me about. When I was able to get up, I looked over and saw my wife standing on the beach, pointing at my son. Slowly I made out her words: "He's hurt!" She was pointing and I was trying to wipe the water from my eyes to focus. I looked at my son. He was standing upright, holding his arm. That was when I saw it. His arm was bent at the elbow, but bent the wrong way. I ran to him and saw the bulge on his elbow. I saw his face: the pain, the fear. The exhilaration in me turned sour in my stomach, and after that it was simply one step after another in a desperate, terrified fog.

The arm was eventually set without surgery, and, after a couple of difficult months of rehab, my son was good as new. My wife and I talked to him at various points in the months that followed about what had happened and his feelings. But the one emotion that I never mentioned having was the joy I felt before that last wave hit. It felt wrong to associate joy with such a frightening experience. I couldn't have imagined discussing it with my wife, let alone my son. After about a year, however, he and I were in the car, and it came up. I don't remember what prompted it, but there it was. I confessed that riding those waves had brought me a joy that I had not felt for a very long time. We stopped at a light, and I looked across at him cautiously. He turned to meet my gaze. A smile slowly edged up his face, and he nodded. "I know," he said, "me too." That was it. That was all we needed to say. Even though we both knew the result of that day, we could not deny the exhilaration that had preceded it. Joy had unfortunately brought us just a little too close to danger. But why had it? Why does joy often come when we are nearest to the edge of fear?

For us as human beings, fear is a complicated phenomenon. Much of why I began to study fear was an attempt at unraveling these mysteries, both for myself and my patients. As a psychologist, I sat every day listening to the stories of suffering caused by fear, and I began to see that fear was far more devastating than I had ever imagined.

Unlike other animals' fear, human fear comes in strange shapes and sizes. Something about who we evolved into has dramatically changed the role that fear plays in our lives—not only personally, but historically and societally as well. Rather than the trusted ally in survival that fear is for other animals, fear, for us, is often something we guard against.

In 1933, Franklin Delano Roosevelt cautioned us about fear. He spoke those now famous words in his first inaugural address to a nation crippled by despair and longing for hope. The recovery from the economic collapse of 1929 had stalled, and FDR knew that, if the country was to get out of its current economic morass, it needed to come to terms with the emotional underpinnings of such a collapse. FDR understood that fear played a prominent role in both the despair and the potential for recovery. He knew that, at times, fear cripples and corrodes, even if the perception of danger is ultimately irrational. FDR spoke to this quite eloquently when he said, "…let me assert my firm belief that the only thing we have to fear is fear itself—nameless, unreasoning, unjustified terror that paralyzes needed efforts to convert retreat into advance."

This paralysis of which FDR spoke is something most of us have experienced at some point in our lives. This is what countless self-help books attempt to free us from. But what I have come to wonder about is why fear is so difficult for us in the first place, and how it became so different for us *Homo sapiens.* To find answers to these questions, I looked first to my patients. From there, I began a long journey that took me deep into the history of how we became who we are today. Neurobiology, history, sociology, evolutionary biology, cognitive science, psychoanalysis, and comparative psychology all contribute to what I am exploring here. This book is not a "how to," but a "how come?"

There is a scene that plays out daily on any street corner. I've watched it many times. A toddler dawdles on a sidewalk. His mother waits nearby with an empty stroller, evidently ready to go home. She has said a dozen times, "Come on, it's time to go, we have to go…ready to go?" And then those terrifying words just seem to come out of nowhere: "I am leaving." Just three simple words in that hauntingly singsong melody, "I am leaving." Immediately, the child freezes, turning, locked on his mother as she takes that first step away from him. And without missing a beat, the child screams, "No! Wait!" He comes running to her side, frightened, obedient, compliant.

Beginning early for us in tiny moments of relational fear, our core experience around uncertainty shapes not only our personal psychology but the very fabric of our society. So much so that it is no wonder great thinkers such as Alan Watts and Paul Tillich have described our time as an age of anxiety.[1]

More than fifty million people in the US ages eighteen to fifty, or 19 percent of the total adult population, are estimated to suffer from some form of diagnosable anxiety disorder during any given twelve-month period.[2] These statistics include generalized anxiety, panic disorder, obsessive-compulsive disorder, phobias, social anxiety, agoraphobia, and PTSD. This already high proportion jumps to about 31 percent when we look at lifetime statistics. To my thinking, that is near epidemic proportions. And when we consider the number of us who suffer from high levels of anxiety, but who fall just short of the diagnostic criteria, the statistics become even more startling.

Needless to say, a great deal of our personal and medical resources are going into managing and treating the effects of anxiety and its ultimate source, fear. Emergency rooms are filled with panic-disordered patients mistakenly believing they are having heart attacks, and the pharmaceutical industry is getting rich medicating our generalized anxiety.

But in addition to these symptoms and costs, there is a more subtle and pernicious effect that haunts so many of us. Vast areas of our lives are unavailable to us due to this fearfulness: our freedom is constricted, our well-being is diminished, and our ability to actualize ourselves—to bring forth who we are and who we wish to become— is lost to us. And as we will come to see, one of the particularly problematic aspects of fear is that it possesses a marvelous ability to operate within us unseen.

This is what I came to witness with one of my patients, by the name of Tim.[3] When he first came to see me, Tim seemed quite content. He was comfortable in his current job and had a good relationship with a woman he liked; the only conflict they had was related to his lack of ambition. Unlike his girlfriend, Tim was content; he didn't pursue new work opportunities or look for ways to express himself, either personally or professionally. This difference was a source of conflict between them. So much so that she made him promise to go into therapy to fix "what was wrong."

Although I value creativity and personal ambition, I do not believe that everyone needs to pursue such interests. To my mind, there is nothing pathological in living one's life contentedly, simply getting by. But that is different from someone taking the path of least resistance because they are afraid.

Up to that point, what I knew about Tim was that he had no interest in pursuing advancement in his career. He specifically told me that, if he did feel that desire, he would pursue it, that it wasn't fear that was holding him back; it was a lack of desire. He said, "What am I supposed to do? I just don't feel it."

This was where we left it, until one day Tim revealed to me that he had not cried in fifteen years. I was struck by a deep wave of sadness and compassion. He told me that he had forced himself not to cry, and that it had worked. The last time he had cried was following a humiliating episode with a girl in high school. What we discovered, as we spent time with his pain, was that when he cut off his feelings of hurt, he also cut off his feelings of desire. Desire, it seems, was what got him into trouble in the first place. Parts of him that sought to protect him from future hurt began to systematically condition him not to want anything. Fear of hurt, humiliation, and pain forged a very particular protection. It was a protection that remained completely out of awareness, and in its invisibility, it was wildly successful.

Given the pernicious life of fear in our society, it is perhaps no wonder that we fight fear on every front. Empowerment gurus and self-help authors have engineered countless systems and programs designed to free people from the vulnerability they face with fear and anxiety. In any number of ways, such leaders in this world of empowerment help their clients and readers face fear head-on and make choices that support other needs besides security.

And let's not forget Oprah and her walk across the hot coals. Although co-opted by the New Age movement, fire-walking has roots that go back thousands of years.[4] Rituals such as this have been woven into Western cultures from ancient Greece to the United States. Regardless of the science behind this phenomenon (which makes it humanly possible), fire-walking is a ritualized experience that gives the participant a new sense of power in relation to fear. People report a renewed vitality in their lives and a freedom to express themselves. Sadly, however, such renewal rarely lasts for long.

Cultural avenues for temporary renewal from fearfulness are present in many forms. From the pride we feel when our valor is rewarded with a medal pinned to our chest, to the answers we find waiting for us in the self-help sections of our book stores (online or otherwise), our culture is rife with possibility. Title after title reveals our longing to acquire courage and to escape our fears. Thousands of books each year promise such relief. And, if there is one thing all these books agree on, it is that fear is the culprit in the loss of vitality and self-fulfillment. Overcoming fear, it seems, has almost universal support in Western society. Emerson himself expressed this as a recipe for life. He wrote, "He has not learned the lesson of life who does not every day surmount a fear."[5] Courage is a commodity we all seem to value.

Following the school shooting at Marjory Stoneman Douglas High School in 2018, we got a first-hand glimpse of the repugnance we feel in relation to the cowering effects of fear. The image of deputy Scot Peterson, an otherwise sound member of the sheriff's department, standing frozen outside the entrance to the school while children inside were being killed was both shockingly flagrant and sadly understandable.

What intrigues me about courage, and the lack of it, is not whether it works in overcoming fear, or whether it is something we can acquire, but instead, why it has become necessary in the first place. Why has our culture, and countless cultures before it, built so many rituals to support the attainment of courage? Courage, it seems, is a bit like a winter coat. Although it might be quite attractive, we certainly wouldn't own it if it weren't so damn cold. What is it about fear that requires such drastic countermeasures? Isn't fear designed to alert us to what is dangerous? Why would fear, something so crucial to our survival, evolve within us to become such a threat?

Chapter One

What Fear Can Do to Us

"Our deepest fears are like dragons guarding our deepest treasures."

—Rilke

Every so often, a patient of mine asks me about the turtles. I have a lot of them. They sit on several shelves in my office, along with my books. I don't remember how I started collecting them, but I do remember when I got the first one.

I was cleaning out my mother's apartment after she died. There it was, in a little curio cabinet. I remembered this turtle from my childhood. It was a goldish-colored metal, and its shell opened to reveal a hidden compartment. I took it down from the shelf and sat wondering what I might find inside. Would it be some clue to my mother's life or to my childhood? Perhaps something long forgotten: a lock of hair, an antique ring, an old penny. When I opened it, however, I was surprised to find it empty. I think I was disappointed, but it is hard to know, given the grief I was in.

When patients ask me about the collection, I am open to talking about it. I have never told anyone about the connection to my mother; I simply say that I started collecting them a while back and that I find turtles quite fascinating. I often say something about how they remind me of people, the shells we have and the ways we hide.

I believe I said something like this to April. She and I had been working together in psychotherapy for a relatively short time, maybe six months, when she asked about them. Most likely, before I told her what the turtles meant to me, I inquired about what she imagined.

In depth psychotherapy, the relationship of patient and therapist is both real and imagined. It is real in that, as a therapist, I work to be present and emotionally truthful. But it is imaginary in that, as a therapist, I come to inhabit roles for my patients—and they for me—that are infused with subjective imaginings. This, in the work of depth psychotherapy, we call transference and countertransference.

What we have discovered as clinicians over these 120 years, since Sigmund Freud and Carl Jung turned our attention to the unconscious, is that patterns from our early development tend to be the raw materials from which we build our imaginative perceptions of others.[6] These "projections" are something we all experience. In essence, they are the building blocks of our subjectivity.

In using the term *imaginative* to describe this type of cognition, I am highlighting a model of the mind that we will be exploring more in Chapter Three. Imagination, in this model, is less of a *conscious* creative act and more of an *unconscious* one. It is something creative that is continually being *produced within our minds*, something we only tangentially participate in. The psychologist Steven Pinker refers to this as the basis of intelligence, a process of "metaphor and combinatorics."[7] So, when April became curious about why I have a collection of turtles, it was an opportunity for us to understand just a little bit more about her and where her mind spontaneously would take her.

April is a thirty-two-year-old single woman who has lived her entire life in New York City. She grew up with a narcissistic father who was quite emotionally demanding. Currently, she works as an actuary in the insurance industry.

My experience of April is difficult to describe. She is pleasant and attractive, in a down-to-earth sort of way. She is socially adept, but there is a remote quality to her that is always present. There are moments in the midst of her speaking when she will look downward in such a way that her eyelids seem to close. These are moments of quiet distance in which April seems far away, on what she calls her "secret island." So I wait. I wait for her to return. And when she does, it is almost as if she is surprised to find me still there. That's when I see the fear.

April grew slowly into her fear, it seems. Little by little, her father's expectations, demands, and subtle coercion began to shape a pattern of threat recognition around love and relationship. She slowly receded from dating and romance, and by the time I first met her, she had been alone for a number of years.

As I began my explorations to understand these relational movements of fear and defense, I quickly discovered that human beings seem to be the only animals that suffer with fear in this way. I am not talking about fear limiting behavior or restricting exploration; that is a part of fear's arsenal that serves all animals, protecting them from harm. I am talking about a deeper impact upon our humanity, some way in which fear seems to turn against us. What we will see, going all the way back to the first moments of life, is that there is something quite unique about us as human beings, and that this difference alters the way fear operates within us.

The Birth of Fear

As babies, we come into the world utterly helpless. Not only do we rely on our caregivers for protection and physiological nurturing; we rely on them for more complex psychological development as well. This is where we part company with other animals. Later in this book, we will drill down a bit deeper into the particulars of how evolution brought us to this place, but for now, let it suffice to say that *Homo sapiens* come into the world with significantly higher degrees of dependence than other animals, including our primate relatives. Coming into the world with vulnerability such as this opens us up to a broad range of potential psychological troubles. And yet, our vulnerability and dependence often go unnoticed—that is, until something goes wrong.

Following the bombings of London in World War II, countless children and infants were orphaned and housed at the London Foundling Hospital. Working there at the time was an Australian physician and psychoanalyst by the name of Rene Spitz.[8] What struck Spitz initially was how quiet it was in the nursery at the hospital. Even though these many infants, under one year old, were abandoned and alone, none of them were crying. Spitz began to study these infants and started the world on a path toward understanding the needs of infancy and the importance of maternal love.[9]

Spitz came to understand what happens to a baby that is systematically deprived of love. Severe neglect, such as these infants experienced over many months, began to turn them into mere shells of human beings. The physicians called this condition "anaclitic depression," a depression that occurs in the first year of life, stemming from trauma such as this.

To get a better idea of what these withered infants were like, I recommend that you Google the videos of Rene Spitz and the "Foundling Infants." You will see how the life force within these young human beings receded back into some deep reservoir, and all that was left was dark and vacant. These neglected infants no longer responded to the world with need, and no efforts from the world seemed to get through to them.

Without much difficulty, we can see something of April's struggle in these infants: when the world is too threatening, retreat is the only answer. And if retreat is physically impossible, then isn't it amazing that our nervous systems found a way to retreat while remaining physically present? Of course, these infants did not fare as well as April. Extreme forms of deprivation, such as these infants experienced, are hard to come back from. But what is similar is that, beginning in the first moments of life, our well-being is in the hands of others. And if those others do not handle us with love and care, we suffer deeply. Ours is a dependence from which there is no safe retreat.

One of the marvels of childhood development is the way in which children are able to remain aligned with their caregivers, no matter what happens to them. Not only are we biologically programmed to maintain physical proximity to our caregivers, an aspect of what we call "attachment," but human attachment also psychologically programs us to "love and trust" our parents. When "bad" things happen to us as children at the hands of a parent, it is not the parent who gets the blame. Children have a simple logic: "If I am good, I get the candy, and if I don't get it, I must be bad." Ronald Fairbairn, an early psychoanalyst following Spitz, called this the moral defense.[10] The parent is viewed by the child as morally superior. If actions of the parent cause pain to the child, or if the child fails to receive what they need, the child places blame for this, not on the parent, but on themselves. "It must be what I deserve." In this way, the child is able to maintain a better connection to the caregiver. If they take the badness into themselves, then the parent is preserved as good, and this allows the child to stay more easily connected. It's hard to love a bad parent. It is easier to be bad and love a good one.

What I want to highlight here is that we have evolved ways to stay connected even when a parent is highly dysfunctional. This is both amazing, from an evolutionary engineering standpoint, and extremely sad, from a human point of view. Too often, those who should be protecting us become those who threaten us most; a childhood that is designed to be full of play becomes a perfect petri dish for the cultivation of fear.

Playing Matters

Play, fear, and vitality are meaningfully interwoven within the animal world. Research on species as diverse as tortoises and rats indicates that, when play is absent from the life of an animal, well-being becomes compromised.[11] For human beings, there are further indications that absent or constricted play is associated with higher levels of psychological dysfunction.[12] And in considering the causes of constricted play, fear emerges as the primary culprit.

In one series of studies,[13] researchers looked at the backgrounds of men who were incarcerated for homicide. Two findings stand out. In the homicidal group, there was significantly more physical abuse than in the control group—and with abuse comes fear. What is even more surprising, however, is that the homicidal group also had a startling absence of play reported in their childhoods.

The lead researcher on this study, Stuart Brown, later became aware of the work of Jane Goodall and contacted her to share his work. He had become intrigued by the 1976 report on Passion and Pom, the mother and daughter chimpanzee duo who systematically and cooperatively murdered and cannibalized infant chimpanzees in their community. Jane Goodall related to him that Passion and Pom had both experienced ineffectual mothering and exhibited profound distortions in their play as juveniles.[14]

In thinking about these curious findings, we need to be as parsimonious as possible. The simple existence of a correlation between the absence of play and murderous tendencies does not in any way prove that they are causally linked. But, for our purposes here, it is meaningful to consider the importance of play in mammalian life, and further, to wonder about the ways in which play is part of a much larger symphony in which we negotiate our relationship to fear.

Play and Risk

For most juvenile animals, play takes shape primarily in the form of rough-and-tumble. For human beings, rough-and-tumble is just one part of a wider spectrum of play that includes object play, symbolic/ fantasy play, rough-and-tumble, and games with rules.[15] Risky play, related to rough-and-tumble, is generally identified as any play that brings the participant within a meaningful distance of danger. This is the type of experience I described in the introduction, riding waves with my son. It is often divided up into play with heights, play in proximity to dangerous objects, and play with speed.[16] We climb a tree to the thinnest branch that can hold us, walk along the edge of a narrow ledge, play with fire, or ride our bikes as fast as we can down a hill and then take our hands off the handlebars.

Research on this form of play has been important in understanding how to keep children safe and define policy. Recent trends have moved our families and communities toward a dramatic reduction in what we view as potential risk for children. Much of this has to do with increased supervision, and as we all know from our own childhoods, increased supervision means decreased fun. But the increased safety is also a function of a reinvention of outdoor play equipment, replacing the hard impact of metal and concrete from the past with the padding of a softer landing.

Recent research by Scott Cook of the University of Missouri looked not just at what children do in risky play, but also at what they feel.[17] In this research, risky play is not just the result of inadequate risk assessment, attention-seeking, or an impulse for self-harm. It is a developmental experience of exhilaration that has emotional and biological validity for the developing child. Supporting this is the neurodevelopmental research on adolescence that has found very particular areas of brain development that are promoted by risk-seeking behavior.[18]

One element that stands out in research on risky play is that there is an edge between safety and danger that best promotes exhilaration. As we might imagine with my son, when he turned and saw a wave forming that was far bigger than the six we had ridden previously, he froze. The balance between safety and danger had been crossed. Fear held him, and he braced himself. Unfortunately, he was no match for the strength of the wave. The only way to survive that wave was to playfully surrender to it.

Fear has a constrictive effect on play, and yet dangerous play, play on the edge of fear, brings with it an evolutionary derivative of joy.[19] Has this strange evolutionary cocktail been mixed to help us learn how to more easily approach fear? Is it an effort to calm our inherited terror by giving us a sense of mastery over fear? Or is it possibly a joy that comes when freedom from fear becomes possible?

A clue to this connection lies with our animal relatives and their use of rough-and-tumble play. Rough-and-tumble is the rolling, wrestling, and pinning that we see in animals from mice to puppies to human beings. Early understandings of play such as this stressed its value as an educative tool. This is the model of play fighting as preparation for real fighting. Today, understandings of play fighting center on notions of relational learning.[20] What stands out in these theories is the idea that, through rough-and-tumble play, animals learn to adapt to unpredictable *social circumstances* with flexibility—an education in assuming varying social roles. And in these changing roles, stress and fear are managed within non-threatening situations. Additionally, these social roles pivot on the axis of social dominance. In rough-and-tumble play, juveniles learn to assume both submissive and dominant positions.[21]

It is this last element that I believe is most important for us in understanding the connection between risky play and fear. There appears to be something quite meaningful in our relationship to submission—so important, perhaps, that these behaviors of play in the realm of dominance and submission have become hardwired into the DNA of mammals, including us. And, as we will come to learn, our fear of being dominated by another of our species is so terrifying to us that we will do anything to avoid it.

As many of you might be aware, animals held in captivity are prone to develop behaviors called stereotypies. These are repetitive movements without apparent function or purpose. Examples range from the pacing of a large cat in a relatively small enclosure to the chewing behaviors of a horse on the wood of his stall. Zoo personnel have come to use these behaviors as markers to identify situations in which animals might be experiencing "poor animal welfare." This might include situations in which animals are severely neglected, abused, or exposed to unhygienic conditions. The issue of stereotypies is no small matter. It is estimated that eighty-five million animals worldwide suffer from this condition.

What emerges from the research, however,[22] is evidence that stereotypies occur not only in toxic environments, but in more neutral environments as well.[23] This is not to say that this second group of animals is free of distress, but that the distress is not always so evident. There is some thinking that stereotypies are a result of the thwarting of the animal's natural instincts. And, of course, all captive animals are subject to this. What could be more of a natural instinct than to be free? We find this thinking not only in animal welfare, but in prison welfare as well. Activists fighting inhumane treatment in prison systems have spoken out against the use of excessive isolation.[24] The common denominator within these varied environments is lack of freedom, social inhibition, and sensory deprivation.

Fear not only robs us of our capacity to play; it also holds us in a form of confinement that restricts the freedom of our minds. Fear, metaphorically, is the great captor, and—just as in more literal forms of captivity—its effects are devastating to our vitality and well-being.

Submission and Freedom

"Never tap out." This is a phrase that came from a patient of mine who wrestled for sport beginning in high school. She came to see me when she was thirty years old. Her name was Janie, and her experience with wrestling came to be quite meaningful to our work.

Never tapping out, as I came to learn, was what Janie's high school coach had demanded of her. Tapping out was like saying "uncle." It was an admission of mental defeat, a recognition of fear's power to make you run away. Her coach required that his wrestlers never give up. He would say, "You keep fighting until you can't fight anymore. You don't let yourself get pinned."

For Janie, never tapping out represented an unconscious refusal to admit that someone had the power to make her submit. What I came to learn was that this battle against submission began early in her relationship with her mother. Being apart from her mother was unbearable for Janie, even up to her teens. Early on in our work, Janie talked endlessly about how wonderful her mother was, how caring, thoughtful, and giving she was. Janie's mother's love, however, was narcissistically suffocating, fostering helplessness, dependence, and ultimately, submission. Although I could easily see there was something unhealthy in this dynamic, it took Janie a long time to realize this.

Submission, we discovered, was a complicated experience for her. This is true for all animals, but particularly so for human beings. In my view, it is a strong contender for what we as a species might fear most—not only biologically, but psychologically, as well. In speaking of the experience of submission, it is impossible to conceive of it without invoking an "other." We submit *to* someone, or because someone demands it of us. It is what happens when a person persuasively asks that we hand ourselves over to them. And it is activated in us equally in experiences of "love" and domination.[25]

In submission, there is something being done to us that overpowers our humanity and renders us mere animals fighting for our lives. We are, however, a very particular kind of animal—one that appears to be sensitive to loss of freedom, not just in terms of physical confinement, but in terms of psychological confinement as well.

Related to the human experience of submission is the neurobiological response of tonic immobility. Under extreme stress and fear, when the life of an animal is at stake, its nervous system can literally shut down. In laboratory settings, this experience can be induced by repeatedly flipping a frightened animal onto its back and holding it there. Eventually, the animal will stop fighting and go limp. It is a shutting down of the nervous system. The evolutionary value of this particular response to trauma is worth considering. From one angle, it is a form of playing possum, of fooling a predator into thinking that you as prey are dead. But it is also, potentially, a way to keep the nervous system from becoming overwhelmed by terror.

As human beings, we have our own version of this. It happens during violent sexual attacks and is sometimes called rape paralysis. Similar to tonic immobility, it is a fear response that occurs at the height of threat, when escape is impossible. In some cases, this type of fear response has prevented the completion of the act—cases in which, without the fight and violence of the act, the rapist loses interest or is unable to finish.

Not surprisingly, victims of rape who have experienced this form of paralysis feel shame about what has happened to them. The inability to stop this terrible thing from happening, the feeling of responsibility, and the sense of worthlessness that comes naturally when someone is treated with such contempt, all form the bedrock of this shame. The shame attached to this protective neurobiological strategy is cited as one of the reasons victims of sexual assault do not come forward to report what has happened. Loss of freedom, powerlessness to stop abuse, and the experience of someone being robbed of their personal sovereignty combine to make them feel less than human.

Survival operates for us in neurobiological systems far removed from our higher-level cortical brains. And when our survival is at stake, our biology willingly sacrifices our dignity and well-being for our continued existence. Fear and the biological longing for survival promote both our resistance to submission and our eventual acquiescence to it. On the one hand, when the demand for submission is upon us, we will fight tooth and nail to resist being harmed, restrained, or confined. On the other hand, when our fear becomes overwhelming, and when both escape and resistance fail, our nervous system opts for some form of neurobiological shutdown. In other words, our survival instincts resist being dominated, physically and psychologically, until they don't. If fighting against physical and psychological submission begins to threaten our existence, then our biology has no other option but to submit.

For a child living in a psychologically toxic environment, escape is impossible. The utter and absolute dependence of a child upon a parent requires that the child maintain a "positive" relationship with that parent, regardless of how much pain they experience in doing so. And if submission is required, then little else is possible. Eventually, the will to resist submission yields to the pressure of fear and the need to maintain connection with the parent. This is when our mind begins to pull us away from life.

Like a turtle, my patient April pulled her head inside her shell, away from danger. The submission she offered to her father was in form only, devoid of what was most real in her. As a defense, this worked quite well. The problem, however, is that, when such defenses become mobilized chronically, they tend to get stuck. April carried with her the imprint of a fear that kept her distant and remote. Unlike a turtle's responsive relationship to environmental threat, April lost the ability to poke her head back out again. Fear had indeed found a way to keep her safe, but the woman who came to my office that first day was also empty and depressed.

April was unable to let anyone see who she was. Deep connection was unavailable to her. She suffered alone. Not only that, but April also lacked awareness of her own needs. The longing to connect, to feel close, was kept from her awareness. The self that she kept hidden remained safe, but profoundly alone. And, as we began to get in touch with her inner world, we found a richness of emotion, self-expression, and vulnerability intermixed with the areas of pain from her early childhood.

Inside her mind was a fragile creativity that she had unconsciously protected for all those years. And, although she kept herself hidden to avoid captivity, her fear became a new prison. Freedom, she and I discovered, came not through avoiding her pain, but through accepting it.

Chapter Two

The Security Alarm System

"Could you be in a state of fear without feeling afraid?"

—Ralph Adolphs

A woman with the initials SM went to a hospital in Los Angeles one day because she was having blackouts. While there, she met a neuroscientist from USC by the name of Antonio Damasio. As he interviewed her, he noted something quite unusual: she reported that she had no fears and, in fact, had never been afraid once in her whole life.[26] What Damasio and his colleagues learned was that SM, for all intents and purposes, was fearless.

SM, it turns out, has a rare condition known as Urbach-Wieth disease. The three primary symptoms of this condition are small pimple-like bumps near the eyes, a hoarse voice, and, most importantly, calcification in select areas of the brain, particularly near the amygdala. What made SM unique to researchers was that, in her case, the calcification that occurs with this condition had completely consumed the amygdala on both sides. Basically, Damasio was face-to-face with a woman who had no amygdala.

No bigger than an almond, the amygdala is located on both sides of the brain. Although the amygdala's specific functioning is debated by neuroscientists, it has been identified in a great deal of research as central to the experience of fear.[27] SM's case gave Damasio a rare opportunity to witness, through its very absence, the amygdala's role in fear. In turn, this case gives us a unique glimpse into what it would be like to live without fear.

SM has an innocent and trusting nature that often gets her into trouble. When the researchers brought SM to an exotic pet store, she was immediately drawn to snakes and spiders without any hesitation. She wanted to hold them and even touched the tongue of a snake. Though great for working with exotic pets, SM's lack of fear has significantly impacted her quality of life.

A number of years ago, SM was assaulted while crossing a dark field at night in a neighborhood known to be frequented by criminals. Yet, even after the assault in that field, the next day, she walked right back through it again. SM is also prone to engaging with strangers, regardless of observable danger signals. Once, in a vacant park at night, she was held up at knifepoint by someone who seemed perfectly safe to her. SM continued to trust men who in the past had harmed her physically, and she still had no sense of apprehension when presented with the possibility of becoming involved again with these dangerous men.

SM is indeed fearless—but, clearly, this is not what we are after when we wish to be free of the limiting effects of fear. SM walks straight into situations that put her life at risk. Without fear, our survival would be difficult to maintain. Whether we like to admit it or not, being scared is sometimes the smartest thing to be.

But what is it that determines whether fear will serve us or betray us? Are there different needs that we have as human beings that determine the value of fear? Is there such a thing as *good fear* or *bad fear*? And most importantly, is our distrust of this protective emotion misplaced?

As a start to answering these questions, I would like us to look a bit deeper into a further piece of research SM agreed to participate in.[28] Up to this point, SM had been taken to haunted houses, shown frightening films, and exposed to dangerous animals, all without any activation of fear. This time, however, researchers slowly changed the ratio of oxygen to CO_2 in the air she was breathing in the lab room, an experiment known as the 35 percent CO_2 inhalation challenge. Within minutes, something began to happen for SM, something she had never felt before. SM began to experience fear.

What this fascinating finding reveals is that SM's lack of fear is not a result of her lacking the ability to feel the emotion of fear. SM doesn't feel fear because nothing is *telling* her to feel fear. Somehow, in the CO_2 experiment, something did tell her to feel fear.

The CO_2 experimental design is often used by researchers in the study of panic. It is a surefire way to induce a strong panic/fear response. What was unique about this experiment, compared to other experiments SM participated in, is that the danger was internal, not external. And this internal signaling of danger was working just fine in SM—even without an amygdala.

Prior experiments for SM were focused through her senses, particularly vision and hearing. This experiment involved a more direct, internal, bodily perception of danger. The monitoring of internal systems of physiological regulation is referred to as "interoception." Evidently, this physiological and neural machinery was working just fine for SM. The neural "module" that actually produces fear was also working fine. SM's case has helped us begin to differentiate the fear *response* from the neural machinery that *interprets* sensory information and monitors for threat, the latter being dependent upon the amygdala.

In the initial experiments with SM, sensory information regarding potential threats traveled from her senses through the corresponding cortical areas, and then on through the amygdala to the midbrain and the motor cortices where aversive actions are initiated. Through this neural pathway, the data are assessed for risk and the appropriate behaviors are initiated: freezing when threats are distant, running when threats are imminent, and fighting when threats are upon us. In the CO_2 experiment, however, the data regarding potential threats does not enter the *senses* to be processed by the higher cortical regions. Instead, this interoceptive data has a kind of hotline that directly triggers the midbrain motoric panic response.

There's a startling lesson here: while the amygdala is critical to fear conditioning and threat detection, it is not the ultimate source of the emotion of fear. Joseph LeDoux championed the amygdala's role in the "experience" of fear,[29] but, according to researchers such as Jaak Panksepp and Lucy Bivens,[30] he fails to give adequate weight to the midbrain's involvement in the experience of fear. This deeper source for fear is supported not only by the CO_2 experiment, but also by "awake brain surgeries" in which a surgeon directs an electrical stimulation to the midbrain and, with this, the surgical patient has a physiological and cognitive experience of fear.

The significance of this is twofold. First, the fact that fear activation occurs deeper within the brain explains some of why fear is so problematic for us. We literally have less neural access to the regions of the brain that generate fear. These deeper fear centers were online for us long before we evolved into *Homo sapiens*. Consciousness, as we will explore more in Chapters Three and Four, is a relatively recent addition, and as of yet, it has not found a way to control fear's effect on us.

The second important element we can glean from this most recent research with SM is that the *emotion of fear* is not the only ingredient in the human recipe for security.

When Fear Isn't Enough

I'm not one of those people who tend to remember lines from poetry or fiction, but a few lines from the novel *The Information*, by Martin Amis, have always remained with me. The narrator is describing his protagonist Richard rising from bed in the morning. Richard, as we are about to learn, is not doing well emotionally.

The narrator describes how he wakes up that day: "He woke at six, as usual. He needed no alarm clock. He was already comprehensively alarmed."[31]

As these lines came into my head one recent morning, I wondered why. What was my mind working on? Did it have relevance for me or just for my book? I remember when I first read the lines, chuckling at their cleverness—like a good clue to the Sunday crossword. But something beyond the cleverness of these lines seemed to be at work. There was something meaningful about what it means to be alarmed in relation to what it means to be afraid.

Being afraid is more than just the emotion of fear. For its part, fear has a whole repertoire of things it can do. It can cause us to focus our attention, remain motionless, run like hell, fight for our lives, or just withdraw slightly from life. These defensive responses are called *action tendencies*, and every emotion contains a unique blend of them.[32] But we first need to be aware that the activation of the emotion called fear, including these defensive behaviors, is only as good as the system that is detecting and interpreting what is uniquely dangerous to us.

Systems of animal security, in the simplest terms, are built around a capacity to detect threat and initiate defensive behaviors. Each species has evolved unique capacities for detection and response to danger, as well as innate fears that prime the system to what *could* be dangerous. An example of this is seen in the algae octopus. It may surprise you to learn that males have one arm that is significantly longer than the others. This arm, it turns out, is the equivalent to a penis that they insert into the female to deposit their sperm. The arm is long because the female of the species has an inconvenient tendency to strangle and eventually eat the male after he has finished depositing the sperm. The arm's length gives the male a little advantage in getting away from love's embrace.

Evidently, this cannibalistic strategy has proven successful for the overall survival of the species. The adaptation of providing the male with distance via his long arm, although paradoxical, seems to improve the octopi's reproductive functioning and balance within the ecosystem—for, while it is true that the female benefits from the additional nourishment required for gestation, most likely the species would not benefit if every male were caught and eaten with each act of insemination. Males come into the world primed to be cautious of the female during mating; the extension of the arm, along with that innate caution, seems to give the males enough of a head start.

Innate fears and physiological adaptations develop in animals over eons. These fears are perhaps the most vital element in the maintenance of animal security. They correspond to expected dangers and reduce dependence on the vagaries of learning through experience. It is much easier to come into the world knowing what is dangerous than having to experiment or wait for guidance.

Another unique example of species-specific threat detection is found in rats. We all assume that rats and mice come into the world fearing cats. But in actuality, rats and mice only innately fear the *smell* of cats. If you visually present a cat to a juvenile rat that has never learned what a cat looks like, it will not have a fear response. However, if you put a cloth that is saturated with cat odor into a cage with that same novice juvenile, it will innately have a fear response and attempt to get away from that smell.[33]

As strange as this may seem, this adaptation makes a great deal of sense. Fearing the smell of cats innately will keep a rat or mouse from entering or remaining in a space that a cat has recently frequented. Avoidance of cat territory is more supportive of survival than innate fear of the sight of a cat. For, as we know, cats are very attracted to little mice on the run, and it only takes one accidental meeting for it to be too late. Between rats and cats, there is very little room for safe experimentation.

For most mammals, as we mentioned, security is maintained through a complex neural and behavioral experience in which a threat is perceived and defensive behaviors are initiated.[34] The first step in this process of maintaining security is the perception of danger.

Information is continually being fed into the brain; if and when something threatening is perceived, activation of fear occurs. This security equation is similar to the equation that operates security systems in homes and businesses. We usually only become aware of these security systems when we hear an alarm go off. But beneath any alarm is a system that monitors the environment for certain specific changes that are deemed worthy of an alarm response. The effectiveness of any security system lies in the precision and accuracy of this monitoring system. We need to be assured, if we are monitoring for fire, for example, that our system knows what to look for and is sensitive enough to trigger an appropriate alarm response.

In terms of human security, our brains have the capacity to differentiate between different kinds of threat and to initiate unique responses specific to the threat that is perceived. For instance, if you see your child about to run into traffic, you might have a very different fear response than you would if you were walking down an unfamiliar dark street at night. The same emotion, fear, is capable of eliciting different security responses.[35] Even the fear response that causes freezing, one of the primary means of maintaining security, has subtle variations depending on the circumstances. An *attentional freeze* is designed to exact a razor-sharp focus for a distant threat, while a *hiding freeze* allows the nervous system to quiet and prepare to run again. One might even include in this list the "submission" response of tonic immobility that we explored in the last chapter, in which our non-conscious brains can shut down the entire nervous system in order to survive.

What does all this mean to us? First, we need to broaden our understanding of human security. The emotion of fear is merely the alarm that triggers defensive behaviors. But this emotion needs something to activate it. Under most circumstances, our sensory perceptual systems determine the threshold for activating fear. And, as we saw with SM, without a functional pathway to the fear centers of the brain, the emotion of fear will fail to be activated. But reduced activation such as this is not what troubles us most about fear.

No one would argue, I imagine, with the logic of desperately trying to outrun a tornado or escape from physical harm when threatened with a baseball bat. Those signals of danger are highly appropriate and worthy of the activation of fear. But the fear that is activated in obvious situations of danger is much the same fear as that activated in situations that our rational minds might deem relatively safe. A fear response that wisely keeps us from confronting a rude drunk in a bar can also keep us from applying for a job that we are well-qualified for. Although these fears are qualitatively and quantitatively different, the emotion is fundamentally the same. In each of these situations, something we perceive is processed in relation to our past experience. Signals are sent to the fear centers of the brain, and one of many types of fear response is initiated. This could be a vague sense of dread or an active attempt to flee.

How is it that benign or even beneficial situations come to trigger a fear response? What happens in our brains and minds to create such an unreliable system of threat assessment? Shouldn't something as important as our security have a system that is rational and reliable?

Finding answers to these intriguing questions, as we will see, will not only help us understand the peculiarities of human security, but also lead us to a deeper wondering about the very foundations of our humanity.

> Note: *From this point forward, when referring to the comprehensive security system of threat perception, emotion, cognition, and aversive behavior, I will use the word "Fear" in capitalized form. If I am referring to just the emotion, I will use the word "fear" in lowercase form.*

Chapter Three

When Fear and Imagination First Met

"Fear is not the adrenaline rush. It's that helpless feeling of being alone in the dark."

—Travis Fahs

A patient named Ella came in one day and told me her radiologist had found something suspicious on a recent x-ray. The x-ray was ordered to try to understand the source of a mysterious pain she was experiencing in her lower back. Ella was clearly upset and worried. Her grandfather had died of lung cancer, and Ella had been a smoker for many years before she quit. The fear of cancer was very close to the surface for her.

My first feeling for Ella was concern. I cared a great deal for her, and as she spoke, I worried that maybe she did have cancer. A series of vague images began to fill my mind. I imagined us dealing with the pain and despair. A frightening future flashed before my eyes. I wondered what this would mean for her. What kind of a final chapter would this be? Ella had suffered a great deal in her life and had finally begun to find some peace.

As Ella told me what she was experiencing, I could see how frightened she was. I could also see her imagination, just like mine, kicking into high gear. She began to recount all the tiny symptoms and physical sensations that she imagined were evidence of a cancer she was now about to face—the fatigue, the moments of dizziness, the insomnia the night before, the lack of appetite, a tenderness in her abdomen, stiffness in her neck, shortness of breath. And even though there was no conclusive evidence, Ella just kept repeating, "It could be; I was a smoker; it could be cancer." And of course, Ella was right. It could be.

Aristotle was perhaps one of the first to give voice to the phenomenon that had gripped Ella when he said, "Let fear, then, be a kind of pain or disturbance resulting from the imagination of impending danger, either destructive or painful."[36] The relationship of Fear to imagination that Aristotle was proposing brings front-and-center the question we arrived at in the last chapter related to perception. Fear, we discovered, is an emotional alarm that requires some form of activation. For the most part, this comes from sensory cues signaling danger. But now we are faced with another question. Can fear be triggered by imagination? And if so, as we saw with Ella, can we ever know for sure whether our fears are realistic?

Certainly our fears feel real, but are they? Our appraisal of what is scary is highly unique to each of us, regardless of how similar we may be. What I am afraid of is both similar to and different from each of you, no doubt. It is not a consideration of whether one perspective is more accurate or valuable than another; it is just to note that our individual fears are subjectively different. And even though there are a great many shared fears, our *experience* of those fears appears to be infused with something unique to each of us—what Aristotle was calling "imagination." Threat assessment, then, is not the internalization of objective reality, but an amalgam of sensory experience and our personal, imaginative coloration.

The Boogeyman in the Closet

Infants and children seem to go through fairly predictable stages of fear. Moreover, research indicates that these stages are consistent across cultures.[37] We can glean from this that innate fears appear to have offered us an evolutionary advantage. This fact is interesting enough, but even more fascinating is the possibility that these innate, cross-cultural fears still have relevance for us today.

Understanding the natural unfolding of fear throughout infancy and childhood dates back to 1897, when G. Stanley Hall, the first president of Clark University and one of the pioneers in child developmental research, conducted the first systematic study of children's fears.[38] What he saw then is quite similar to what we see today. At about eight months of age, and continuing until a child is approximately two or three years old, infants fear strangers, particularly men. This fear does not seem to be different when children are cared for communally or in familial isolation with their mother.

A second fear that emerges developmentally is fear of separation. This, not surprisingly, occurs as an infant begins to explore away from his or her mother, at around twelve months, and continues until about two or three years of age. This manifestation is easily recognized at bedtime, but it is also present on the playground, when a toddler begins to explore in ever-widening arcs away from his or her parent. At some point, they look back to make sure they can still see their parent, and most importantly, to make sure that their parent hasn't abandoned them.

The third innate fear that young children all seem to pass through is the fear of monsters and demons. So many of my patients have memories of worrying about the Boogeyman. For some, the monster was under the bed and for others it was in the closet. But what is important to note about this developmental stage of fear, as distinct from the other two I mentioned, is that the object of dread is being conjured up in the imagination. This seems to correlate with the advent of more sophisticated cognitive capacity.

The innate nature of these fears tells us something important about what threats were present for us throughout the course of evolution. The very helplessness of the infant and child demanded proximity to the caregiver. Also evident is the apparent threat that infants faced from other humans outside the closest circle of family. Finally, as children grew older, they learned to be afraid of unseen predators: predators or monsters that they knew existed—in the closet, under the bed. It was evidently prudent for them to keep the possible existence of these predators in mind, even if they couldn't actually see them.

Although most of these childhood fears seem to lessen by adolescence, there is one fear that remains with us long into adulthood—at least metaphorically.

When Night Falls

It's hard to imagine how afraid we once were as a species. How many nights we must have lain awake, unable to close our eyes, staring out into the dark. Waiting. Watching. Futilely attempting to discern shapes and forms—shades of black upon black, like some kind of mocking modernist painting. And if we did eventually see something coming out of that darkness, a feline predator perhaps, we knew instantly that it was too late. The dark held mortal dangers, and it appears that we have not found a way to purge this traumatic memory from our DNA.

In thinking about the evolutionary basis of our fear of the dark, we need first to be aware that *Homo sapiens* were not the toughest kids on the block. The fact that we came to dominate the planet is not a testament to our ability to physically defend against predators and other threatening species, but rather, a function of our ability to adapt and outsmart.[39]

Large predatory cats such as lions have always lived near hominids.[40] Recent research suggests that feline predators are much more likely to attack after dusk and in low-light moon stages. And, according to some, lions were at one time the most widely distributed mammal in the world. Clearly, the threat from nocturnal predators ranks high in our ascription of danger to the dark.

In addition, it seems that our "mastery" of fire, 350,000 to 500,000 years ago, was of little help to us in guarding against our vulnerability in the dark. Yes, it kept us warm, kept a few animals away, and did define a place of certainty in the dark unknown, but what could it really do for us in the big picture? It was a tiny spot of orange in a sea of black. Sadly, light never solves the dark. It merely brings it into sharper focus. And scarily enough, that spot of orange becomes a beacon for those who nefariously wish to know where we are.

By its very nature, the dark is problematic due to our inability to see into it. Without sight, humans are at risk from any number of dangers. If you have ever tried to walk with a blindfold, you know what I mean. In the dark, we are vulnerable to running into sharp objects, walking off a cliff, or twisting an ankle on uneven terrain. Even without the threat of predators, the dark demands caution.

I think we have all had the experience of walking down a dark street in an unfamiliar setting and feeling our bodies respond with heightened vigilance. And if, under these conditions, we then hear footsteps behind us, we might indeed be moved to panic, or at least to experience a mild adrenaline rush.

The effects of the dark on our assessment of danger has great potential importance for us in our understanding of Fear. Research related to this has been extensively done by Mark Schaller of the University of British Columbia.[41] In his experiments, subjects were asked to view photographs of men and rate the level of danger that these men posed. As a variable, Schaller and his associate, Steven Neuberg, experimentally manipulated the amount of light present in the lab room while the subjects rated the photographs. From this, they discovered that, when controlling for other variables, perceptions of danger significantly increased under ambient dark conditions.

The dark makes us more afraid with expectations of potential threat. But are these threats real? This is the question that came into focus most clearly for me with my patient Tony. He arrived for his session one morning feeling quite stressed. He had been talking in past sessions about his need for control and how he tried to manage the many plans he had for himself and those he loved. I remember thinking, "He really loves the feeling of control." I realized that I had drifted off into this reverie when Tony startled me by asking me to change the light in the room—specifically, if I could adjust the blinds to make the room brighter. I said that I would be happy to, but that it might be useful to discuss his feelings about the light. As I opened the blinds, he began to tell me about light and dark, and finally, about his methods for falling asleep. Like many individuals, Tony preferred to fall asleep to the sound of the television. But he also preferred to keep all of the lights on. Needless to say, this was challenging for his wife, so they slept separately—Tony in the living room and his wife in the bedroom. I think I said something to him then about his fear of the dark, and he quickly cut me off. "It's not that I'm afraid of the dark, it's that I'm afraid of *what happens to me in my mind* in the dark."

Tony's observation on the dark and the mind sparked a contemplation for me that would eventually become the foundation for this book. Something does indeed seem to happen to us in our minds in the dark. And whether we call it warranted apprehension or paranoid imagining, the dark evokes a phantasmagoria of frights that operate outside of our rational assessment of threat.

Perceiving in the Dark

What we need to acknowledge first is that darkness is a condition of nature that makes it difficult for us to determine risk. Evidently, our experience with the dark has contributed to our innate fear of it. How many thousands of generations of learning were required to etch this fear so deeply into our DNA? No doubt, our fear of the dark has served our survival, but it has also rendered us prone to overreactions in the face of uncertainty. Reasonable support has been found to assert that bullying, gang violence, and tribal warfare all can be significantly attributed to a sense of threat and "perceived vulnerability to danger."[42] And, if there is one aspect of the dark that is inescapable, it is its inherent relationship to the unseen and the unpredictable.

Following from this vulnerability is the recognition that much of what makes us human began in the dark. I am not just referring to our fear of it, but to what this fear inspired in us. Solving our relationship to the dark, I believe, stretched the limits of our brains until one day, perhaps fifty thousand years ago, a tiny glimmer of something new emerged, something we now call *the mind.*[43]

As we noted in Chapter Two, danger is only actionable when it is perceived. This is the problem with the dark; danger might be lying just beyond the reach of our vision, and we might not even know it. Many species have a simple solution for this problem—smell. Nocturnal hunters, as well as prey, often have highly developed olfaction, and with this they pierce the darkness quite well. But in our evolution, we *Homo sapiens* seemed to find ourselves relying on other mutations. For example, we needed to travel greater distances, and because of this, we evolved a revolutionary capacity to walk on two legs. Overall, this shift toward bipedalism brought us to a more upright posture. Multiple systems appear to have contributed to our following this evolutionary course.[44] We moved away from smell to a heavier reliance on vision. Our snout began to retract, and our eyes became set much more centrally on our faces. We acquired stereoscopic vision, an ability to see color, elongation of our legs and shrinking of our pelvis. Together, these changes brought us dramatically toward what we know today to be the human being.[45] But these changes also brought us into a new relationship to the dark, one that required new forms of vision.

One of the most interesting elements of human vision is called "blindsight." Gordon Binsted, from the University of British Columbia, has studied blindsight extensively and describes it as a "second sight." It relates to the existence of a secondary optic nerve that transmits certain types of visual information directly from the eye to the midbrain, the area of the brain that has been identified as capable of instantaneously, and non-consciously, activating defensive motoric responses such as ducking.[46]

In Binsted's research, subjects with cortical blindness—in other words, with functional retinas, but dysfunctional vision centers near the back of the brain—were able to detect peripheral objects even though they lacked primary vision. This means that the midbrain was able to respond defensively to potential threats without conscious awareness.

Blindsight, once thought to be a secondary neural development following the loss of cortical vision, is now understood to exist, on some level, for all of us. And if Binsted is right in his hunch about the evolution of this secondary visual defensive system, then it would be a defensive system that developed as a step toward solving the problem of unseen aerial danger—in other words, the dark.

Another area of invisible threat that needed to be solved was the realm of infection and poisoning from putrid, toxic, or rotting substances. Somehow, along the evolutionary path, we developed the emotion of disgust, to help us "see" these invisible enemies.[47] Similar to blindsight, disgust is capable of identifying invisible threats and activating motoric behaviors that keep us away from the danger.

As we might imagine, the avoidance of putrid, toxic, or poisonous substances was vital to our survival. The fact that we developed an emotional module specifically to deal with these forms of danger is quite remarkable. Our senses had to learn which smells and sights indicated the existence of this type of danger. It is not that we *see* the actual danger, the microbes, but we see and smell what indicates the possible existence of dangerous microbes. Quite impressive.

As we can begin to see, the problem of unseen danger has had a significant effect on the evolution of human threat detection systems. But more than this, the unseen and the unknowable appear to have shaped the very nature of our minds.

The Evolution of Imagination

In 1987, Alan Leslie, Distinguished Professor of Psychology at Rutgers University, asked an important question regarding the evolutionary necessity of pretend play. He wondered why the human being, so dependent upon a *logical appraisal of reality*, would spend so much time in childhood developing the capacity for pretend play.[48]

In answering the question of the relevance of pretend play, Leslie presented an elegant description of the subtle cognitive shifts that occur in the act of pretending. He called this shift "decoupling," the process of maintaining connection with the meta-representation while loosening the primary representation. An example of this is what happens when we hold a banana up to our ear and pretend that it is an old-fashioned telephone. The primary representation of "banana" is decoupled, separated from its primary meaning. From this, both literal meaning (banana as fruit) and metaphoric meaning (banana as telephone) are able to coexist without disrupting either meaning.

This is what formed the basis for what Leslie called "Theory of Mind." In this model, what the psychoanalyst Peter Fonagy later termed "mentalizing," Leslie posited that the mental mechanism necessary to perform the cognitive shift from one state to another is the same mechanism that allows us to understand the existence of a mind, both our own and that of another. Being able to conceptualize this internal space in which a mind exists is central to what marked the evolutionary movement to becoming human.

In both pretense and the conceptualization of mind, there is a need to bridge the distance between what is known and what is unknown.

For, as much as we might imagine that we know what lies within the mind of another, it does forever remain a mystery. We use what we know of ourselves to "imagine" what might lie within the mind of another.

Related to this is the work done by two cognitive linguists, George Lakoff and Mark Johnson. In 1980, they came together to write what has become a seminal study on the nature of metaphor and its place in culture. The book, *Metaphors We Live By*,[49] puts forth the basic idea that metaphor provides the underpinnings for much of our daily life experience. Abstract conceptual systems are understood through metaphoric processes and, in parallel to this, our metaphors become conceptual. For example, description of things like significance, or the elements of argumentation, is done through a comparison of the abstract to the concrete.

For example:

- *Argument is conceptualized as WAR when we say things like,* "He defended his position by spouting a bunch of theory"; or "His position on this subject is indefensible."

- *Significance as an abstract value is conceived to be LARGE in physical size*: "That is a really big idea"; "He's some kind of big banker"; "She is a really big deal in advertising."

Not only is metaphor a basis for understanding abstract concepts, but, in a parallel manner to Theory of Mind, it appears to have been crucial to the evolution of human intelligence. Using one concept to understand another, and the ability to blend and combine, provided us as humans with a vastly superior potential for adaptation.[50]

A crucial difference between us and other mammalian species, particularly primates, rests upon this adaptive potential that we appear to have acquired about fifty thousand years ago. Because of this, we became the only species to successfully migrate to wildly diverse ecosystems and build eco-specific cultures.

This is the manifestation of the movement Leslie traced from pretense to mind. It is a state in which each of us is capable of containing, in our minds, new worlds and new possibilities. And, as the neuropsychologist Nicholas Humphrey conceived of it, this acquisition of mind bestowed upon us an inner vision that he called "the inner eye." He related this to our evolution and to the value it brought to our ancestors—that first moment when something was different for us.[51] The moment we became *sapiens*; the moment we discovered that we could imagine.

In the context of evolution, this was an extraordinary breakthrough. Think of the benefits this brought to the first of our ancestors—to be able to make realistic guesses about what might lie around a blind corner or, more importantly, what might exist in the mind of another. The way was laid open for a new deal in human social relationships. We acquired sympathy, compassion, trust, and equally, treachery, double-crossing, and suspicion. We learned how to dream and we learned how to imagine.

Let's take a look at where we are so far. About fifty thousand years ago, our minds acquired the capacity to use metaphor. The dark that was unknowable revealed its secrets to us through the associational wonder of speculation and suspicion. We began to predict and imagine what might be waiting in the dark. The realms of prediction grew exponentially with experience. But what was most meaningful in this evolution was the emergence of the concept of the dark as a metaphor for all that was unknowable.

Beginning in the concrete experience of the night, our minds began to conceptualize the abstract notion of uncertainty. And what was applied concretely to the state "when the sun goes down" could now be applied metaphorically to all sorts of things. The world around us, that we thought we knew, took on a double life. In addition to the observable, we soon realized that within each moment of what we thought we knew was a parallel moment of the unknown. Imagination allowed us to fill in the blanks. We acquired the capacity for curiosity, wonder, doubt, and ultimately, distrust.

Seeing into the dark, both concretely and metaphorically, offered us vastly improved abilities to anticipate danger and predict threat. The problem with these abilities, however, is that our security was built, not on an accurate appraisal of reality, but merely on possibility. This is where we can think back to Leslie's wondering about why pretend play became so embedded in children's early development. From this, we might even consider paranoia to be less a symptom of mental illness, and more a testament to the strength of our drive to survive.

If imagining a danger allows us to preemptively protect ourselves, then what difference does it make if that imagining is real or not? Evolution here seems to follow a simple logic. "Better a false positive than a false negative," and "Just because I am paranoid, doesn't mean someone isn't trying to kill me." Imagination became a welcome stand-in for a sense of sight that failed to keep us safe.

> Note: *Similar to the way in which I am noting the difference between the emotion fear and the comprehensive system of Fear, I am differentiating here between two uses of imagination. From this point forward, if I am referring to the comprehensive experience of curiosity, wonder, envisioning, and invention, I will be using the word "Imagination" in capitalized form. If I am referring to just the simple cognitive function of envisioning, I will use the word "imagination" in lowercase form.*

Chapter Four

The Future of Anxiety

"The future is dark, which is on the whole, the best thing the future can be, I think."

—Virginia Woolf

Early in my career as a psychologist, I encountered a patient named Sherry, who was experiencing severe anxiety. She was continually occupied with a vague apprehension that something bad was about to happen. Her principal symptom was a relentless worrying, but this was accompanied by irritability, sleeplessness, and muscle fatigue. She was an obsessive planner and list maker and talked so fast that I could barely keep up. There were no pauses in her speech patterns, and if I wanted to get a word in, I literally needed to interrupt her.

Sitting with her was difficult. She seemed to vibrate and give off an almost electric energy. But what was most surprising, and frustrating, was that she hadn't come for treatment of her anxiety. Rather, at twenty-three, Sherry, a very accomplished young woman, believed that she had so much untapped potential and need for improvement that, if she didn't hurry up, she would literally miss the future that she was "intended" to have. Needless to say, as a rookie therapist, I had no idea how to proceed.

For many of us, anxiety is a crippling ailment that restricts freedom and saps vitality.[52] As we learned in the introduction, anxiety affects nearly one-third of all adults over the course of their lives. This represents a significant portion of our society. Falling under the rubric of anxiety, and included in these statistics, are disorders such as phobias, obsessive-compulsive disorder, panic disorder, and post-traumatic stress disorder. If left untreated, severe forms of anxiety such as these can render someone powerless and victimized. Engagement with life, self-esteem, and self-determination all seem to diminish.

Interestingly, anxiety appears to be something that exists in all cultures. Although current lifestyles in the West have exacerbated anxiety, research suggests that anxiety exists at much the same levels in the East and in developing countries as it does in the United States.[53] The differences that appear cross-culturally are related more to the content and form of anxiety and less to the amount of underlying physiological and psychological distress.

For example, in 1967 in Singapore, a strange anxiety gripped the culture. Many men began to have the intense worry that their genitalia might begin to retract into their abdomen. The worry was so intense and pervasive that clinics were swamped with anxious men afraid that they might contract the "disease" and die. What prompted this epidemic remains a mystery.[54]

But what most of us think of when we hear the term anxiety is what we saw with Sherry. Like Sherry, many of us suffer with what is called generalized anxiety disorder (GAD). This is the type of disorder that most captures the central difference between Fear and anxiety. Whereas Fear is a neurobiological defensive response to an observable threat, anxiety is, instead, an objectless fear, one in which the threat is either vague or hidden.

In my professional experience, GAD is a condition that exists across a broad spectrum, from the more severe forms such as Sherry's to milder forms that don't quite meet the diagnostic criteria. The latter is what many of us live with and is often felt to be the natural outcome of contemporary life.[55] This is the anxiety that is often treated informally with a glass of wine at five o'clock, a couple hits of pot after the kids are in bed, or even a Xanax on a rough day.

Given the high-pressure demands of Western society, it's almost inconceivable to many of us that anyone could be free of this type of anxiety. More so perhaps than depression, anxiety has a vital and non-pathological existence for us. I would be hard pressed to even guess at the number of times I have heard a patient say, "Oh, it's nothing, I'm just a little anxious." It is often said to indicate that the state of distressing arousal and worry they are suffering with is nothing to be concerned about. And while I do believe that these somewhat dismissive statements are often defensive, i.e., a way to devalue or avoid what is beneath the anxiety, there is also something undeniably honest about these words. But Sherry's level of severe apprehension and worry was quite another matter.

All of my attempts to get Sherry to consider her anxiety to be a problem were dismissed. Any time I would ask her to slow down, to sink into the experience of her body, or to get in touch with her inner emotional life, she would resist defiantly. Sherry was someone more devoted to her anxiety than I had ever before encountered. She continued to pressure me to help her reach her potential. She was honestly worried about the future and, particularly, her inability to meet whatever demands might arise.

For my part, being a novice, I would get caught trying to convince her or reassure her that she was above average and had nothing to worry about. I would try to cautiously suggest that maybe something deeper was troubling her, something we didn't yet understand. But all of my efforts fell short. She persisted in tormenting herself with harsh self-criticism that only made her feel more anxious. And when all was said and done, Sherry was certain that her anxiety was warranted.

I remember one day, when I asked her what she imagined would happen to her if she weren't so anxious. She looked at me, smiled, and calmly said, "I think I would probably die."

What's Bugging Us?

Before looking deeper into Sherry's self-prognosis, it might be good to acknowledge that her valuation of anxiety was not totally unfounded. Studies of performance going back more than one hundred years all seem to indicate that anxiety can improve performance.[56] Howard Liddell, an early anxiety researcher, suggested in 1949 that anxiety was the "shadow of intelligence,"[57] and thus an unavoidable accompaniment to an educated and cultured life. David Barlow, who has arguably written the bible on anxiety, goes further in this vein: "Without anxiety little would be accomplished. The performance of athletes, entertainers, executives, artisans, and students would suffer; creativity would diminish; crops might not be planted. And we would all achieve that idyllic state long sought after in our fast-paced society of whiling away our lives under a shade tree. This would be as deadly for the species as nuclear war."[58]

To my mind, Barlow goes too far in this assessment of anxiety's place in society and culture, particularly in his belief that, without anxiety, creativity would dry up. But even in the face of his hyperbole, there is something meaningful we all recognize in what he describes.

Like Sherry, many of us find ourselves in a perpetual state of apprehension and worry, yet still maintain some movement toward accomplishment. Unlike Fear, where the "action tendency" is primarily to pull away from the source of threat, anxiety seems to possess a strange mix of push and pull. Out there in front of us is a threat, and we feel the apprehension. But as Sherry suggests, anxiety strangely possesses some valence that paradoxically moves us toward life and, ultimately, the future.

Into the Future

Looking back as we have with regard to our ancient vulnerability with the dark, we can imagine the benefits an enhanced Imagination had on our ability to improve security. Only a mere fifty thousand years ago, perhaps, we went from reactive fear responses in the moment to preparatory responses that reduced the possibility of risk. In addition to greater sophistication in tool use, long-term solutions such as the accumulation of weapons, the erection of permanent walls, strategic planning, and the establishment of agricultural settlements, emerged as forms of long-term defenses.

Beyond the value these tools and approaches had for us, there was an even more groundbreaking achievement that came with the advent of Imagination. What was truly revolutionary, in my view, and the principal "invention" that most came to define our unique existence as *Homo sapiens*, was the *invention of the future.*

Within our minds, a place opened that allowed us to envision future possibilities and play out probable outcomes. This new vision within the mind's eye is part of what Thomas Suddendorf of the University of Queensland calls "time travel."[59] In his study of the differences between human and non-human animals, Suddendorf has conceptualized this capacity for time travel as what most makes us human. Moreover, I would add, this is the foundation for our sense of self and what allows us to hope and dream.

Much of the research on time travel by Suddendorf and others focuses on the ways in which episodic memory is central to this capacity. Episodic memory is what allows us to create an experiential awareness of ourselves in time and place. For example, "I am living in the twenty-first century; I grew up in the United States, and I plan to take a vacation in February." This is different from what is called semantic memory, the memory of facts, as in, "The capital of New York is Albany."

According to Suddendorf, episodic memory was a prerequisite for time travel. It provided the cognitive framework that allowed us to move "forward" into the future. I see it as an experiential template that allowed us to extend our "felt sense" of the present back into a remembered past and forward into a possible future. With this, we evolved beyond a standard repertoire of responses to a predictable environment—behaviors that evolved over millions of years—and into a new era in which we took evolution into our own hands. More than any other species, we *Homo sapiens* acquired the capacity to *adaptively evolve* and, with this achievement, the future became ours to shape.

What we need to remember, however, is that when Imagination spawned the future, it did so in the service of Fear. The very legitimacy of the future's existence was dependent upon its ability to act as a placeholder for a suspicious mind. For all its potential value, the benign future of unlimited possibility is also the malignant future of infinite terror.

Imagination's success in helping Fear solve the problem of the dark rested upon its predisposition toward suspicion. For this reason, the future that we are so dependent upon appears to inherently carry with it the imprint of impending danger. Further, the future that all of us face is a time and a place that has no substance. The unformed hope that Virginia Woolf expresses in her quote at the start of the chapter mocks us with the reality that who we are in the future is an illusion. In this way, the security of being that we all seek is undermined with every breath we take.

In fostering a solution to the dark of the present, Fear and Imagination brought to life a new form of darkness. And it is this new, future-oriented darkness that I believe contributes to much of the psychological distress that we today call anxiety.

This, to my mind, is why Kierkegaard, Rollo May, and other philosophers have found the source of anxiety to be in the dissolution of existence and meaning. For how can we have a certainty of existence when the future that we so desperately run to slips through our fingers each time we try anxiously to hold it?

Worry as a Bridge to the Future

For most of us, worry is an unavoidable experience in preparing for the future. It is how we manage the what-ifs of life. But worry is also an unreasonable obsession that demands we prepare for the worst, over and over and over again.

What becomes clear when we look more closely at worry is that, when worry is guided by an overactive sense of perceived threat, even if that threat is unlikely or fantastical, the mind seems driven to try and resolve the threat.[60] But, as we all know from experience, worry rarely leads to practical problem-solving.

In looking at theories on anxiety and pathological worry, there is little consensus as to what fosters and maintains worry.[61] One view on the origins of worry suggests that it is a means to avoid the "contrast" between alternating emotional states. From this perspective, people vulnerable to pathological worry would rather maintain the negative state of worry than risk shifts between positive states and negative states. For them, it is not the negative state that is to be avoided, but the *shift* between states.

This view fits quite well with the anecdotal evidence of how we at times buffer ourselves against disappointment. Certainly, we have all found ourselves tempering our excitement for the future by bracing for disappointment. It is essentially what cynicism is all about. "Better to expect the worst, then you won't be disappointed."

A second theory posits that worry is a way to avoid the unwanted emotions implicit in the object of our dread. Given that worry is primarily a verbal/linguistic activity, it differs greatly from the emotional distress of Fear and anxiety. One researcher who supports this model, Thomas Borkovec, describes worry as a form of "talking to oneself."[62] And thus, by occupying the mind with linguistic "worry" activity, the awareness of emotional distress is lessened. This model proposes that worry's value lies in its ability to distract us from our distress.

What I would propose here is that worry, as the primary vehicle for anxiety, is an attempt to reinforce the shaky bridge between the "us" of the present and the "us" of the future. Worry may have come to exist for us as a way to cognitively compensate for the absence of emotional security in a future we cannot control. Could we say, then, that worry is both a symptom of the problem and an imagined solution?

In the years of work with Sherry that followed our somewhat rough beginning, I learned a great deal more about her relationship with her mother. I had known from the very beginning of her therapy that her mom had left the family when Sherry was about five, never to see her again. But what I didn't know was that Sherry had maintained an obsessive imaginative relationship with her mom that centered around a reunion in the future. The imaginings were so real to Sherry that they felt to her like "future memories." As she began to explore these "memories" in sessions, Sherry accessed emotional connections to herself and her imagined future. From these new "bridging" connections, her anxiety transformed into pain and grief. With this, she was able to begin her process of healing.

When Sherry ended therapy, she was still a somewhat anxious woman. No longer, however, was she ruthlessly driven to better herself, and her self-esteem was greatly improved. She laughed more easily, enjoyed the absurdity of life, and found a way to have greater compassion for herself. But what is most important is that when she began to deal with her pain, she was able to reconnect to herself, to her dreams, and to her Imagination. Sherry discovered that she enjoyed volunteering at an adult reading program, and she was amazed at how good it felt to give back to people.

Chapter Five

Fear of Our Own Minds

"To peoples everywhere, darkness connotes evil, threat, and danger."

—Mark Schaller

One of the most notable features of human beings is our lack of accurate self-knowledge. No matter how hard we try, it seems, we fail in this regard. And, whether it is a failure to see our faults or a failure to see our virtues, fail we do. But what is even more distressing is that we have a blind spot about our blind spot.

In thinking about others, whether friend or foe, it is quite easy for us to see the places where accuracy in self-knowledge might be lacking. I am pretty confident that all of us have had the experience of wondering how it is possible for someone to be so blind to themselves. But when it comes to our own self-knowledge, we seem quite comfortably identified with our own self-ignorance.

In speaking of comfort and ignorance, however, I am not implying that we are all happy and at ease in this state—quite the contrary. In my work as a psychologist, I am aware that much of what has brought my patients into therapy seems to pivot on how well they have been able to maintain this knowledge gap. In fact, it is often when life comes crashing down upon us that the false images we have of ourselves begin to crack, and we begin to notice things are not well with us. This was the case with my patient Mason.

I had seen Mason briefly for couples therapy with his boyfriend a few years earlier. They didn't stay in treatment long, just long enough to reset their relationship, give voice to some building resentments, and continue on their way. Even back then, however, I could see that there was something pulling Mason away from himself.

Sadly, just before Mason called me again, his boyfriend, now husband, had had an affair and fallen in love. Mason didn't know what to do or what to feel, so he decided to give me a call.

Even though Mason said he wanted help, I could tell immediately that he had one foot out the door, both in his relationship and in therapy. He made a point of telling me that things were going well for him and he didn't think he needed to come back to therapy. His husband had decided to leave him and that was that. I suggested that we take a few sessions just to see what happens—"No need to commit to anything." He was relieved by the absence of pressure from me and agreed to come.

Like so many other patients in my practice, Mason was driven and successful but ultimately felt an emptiness inside. He wished he could feel something—pleasure, pain—but all he felt was just "okay."

Our work initially centered on feelings of grief and resentment. As much as Mason didn't want to admit it, a part of him was very angry at his husband. And beneath that we found a sadness. Even though they both had occasionally "hooked up" with other people, falling in love was not part of their deal. The few sessions turned into a few more sessions, and soon, Mason allowed himself to feel the sadness, the betrayal, and, most importantly, the hurt. Then, one day, Mason came in and realized that he wasn't angry anymore.

Over the next few weeks, Mason cheerfully reported to me that he was feeling great; everything seemed in place, and his work was going well. Quite predictably, then, Mason came in one day and told me he had run out of things to say. He sat there quietly in the big oversized chair, and that odd sensation came to me again. I could "feel" him edging toward the door. I initially imagined that this feeling of mine was a result of picking up on his reluctance to "go deeper." No crime in that. But in addition to this "feeling," I began to notice the vague outlines of an image in my mind's eye. I saw him running.

I wondered if my feeling and these images were related to a sense that he was running from the pain of his breakup. I decided to cautiously share what I was experiencing with him. When I told him, he looked at me intently and, from his expression, seemed freaked out. He nodded and said, "That is really weird." He went on to tell me that, when he is quiet and has no outside stimulation, he himself has the sensation of running. Even though he might be absolutely still, he runs.

With Mason, the sense of his running seemed to foreshadow what eventually came to be a recognition that some part of him was attempting to distance him from something. It was not that Mason wasn't what he said he was—kind, caring, self-sacrificing, and easygoing—it's just that he was also so much more than that.

As our work progressed, Mason's running pace seemed to slow somewhat. More and more, he allowed himself to wonder about himself. Who he really was, how he came to be this person, and most importantly, what he was actually feeling inside. One day, Mason looked like he had a secret to tell me. With almost a hint of innocent shame, he revealed that for most of his life, he had suffered with the sense that an animal was following him, ready to pounce. He admitted, shamefully, that this was why he was running. The animal, he told me, was more shadow than substance, always in the distance, but it went everywhere with him. Every time he turned around, there it was; yet he could never quite see it clearly.

With time, Mason spoke of how difficult it was for him to have his own needs growing up. His sister, whom he had not spoken of much, was quite depressed in his childhood. She was older and demanded almost all of his parents' attention. Mason was the "happy one," the "good boy," but underneath, there was more. Who he was, it seems, was kept hidden from everyone, including himself. Even his closest friends knew only the outward persona that he presented to the world. One day he said to me, "What will happen, do you think, if I stop running from the animal?" I replied, "Let's find out."

In essence, what happens when Mason stops running is what this chapter is about. Like Mason, many of us have relationships to ourselves that have strong elements of Fear—Fear that pulls us apart and severs our ability to maintain an authentic connection to who we truly are.

Our Two Faces

In 1866, Robert Louis Stevenson published *Strange Case of Dr. Jekyll and Mr. Hyde*. It arrived in a society in which science, medicine, reason, and social decorum were preeminent. Growing out of the Scientific Revolution two hundred years earlier, Victorian Europe was thriving in its capacities for industry and enlightenment. The Industrial Revolution was at hand and the systems of class were neatly organizing humanity into manageable boxes. With the benefit of historical hindsight, however, we can see that the publication of Stevenson's book presaged something meaningful about our culture and our society.

The theme of the story about Dr. Jekyll and Mr. Hyde has become a form of myth, transcending the limits of the novel and extending into the very fabric of our society. But for those of you who have not read the book, let me offer a brief summary.

Unlike the film, the novel is structured as a mystery. There's a shabby door situated on an otherwise clean and lively street. There's an encounter with a brutish man who enters that door. His name is Hyde and, somehow, he seems to have a mysterious power over a respected physician named Dr. Jekyll. There is a murder, and witnesses identify Mr. Hyde. Who is this man and what power does he have over Dr. Jekyll?

With the unfolding of the story, we discover that Dr. Jekyll has found a way to release his "inner man" who longs for pleasure, seeks only to satisfy himself, and feels younger, lighter, and more alive. It is a touching story of a good and devoted doctor who seeks to honor his inner self, but finds that this inner self is capable of inflicting tremendous hurt, and even murder. The story ends with the death of Dr. Jekyll. We are left with the feeling that, if we try to give life to the part of us that we hide from, we will ultimately come to a tragic end.

Reading the story of Dr. Jekyll today makes clear how constricted the Victorian world was. Some have considered the story a clear reference to homosexuality and the need for "bachelors" in Victorian England to hide their desires. For me, however, the book is much broader in its metaphor. It reveals a deep fissure within us, individually and culturally. It is seen in the struggle of good versus evil, noble versus savage, and upper versus lower class. Dr. Jekyll both longs to set his inner self free and struggles to keep this part of him from destroying everything good he has built. For me, these two movements—the longing to reveal what is hidden, and the fear that "the hidden" will harm us—are what our culture and society grappled with as we moved into the twentieth century.

What Science Gave Shape To

In the years following the publication of Stevenson's book, and as Europe was struggling with societal upheaval, a strange new ailment began to emerge. Women (and, to a lesser degree, men) were having symptoms of unexplained paralysis, blindness, and obsession. It was called hysteria, from the Greek word for womb.

Some of the brightest medical minds in Europe were working on this problem. Major advances were being made in France through the work of Pierre Janet and Jean-Martin Charcot using hypnosis.[63] They theorized that something was going wrong in the relationship between the conscious mind and the non-conscious mind. But it was the young Austrian Sigmund Freud who took this a step further and proposed that sexuality was at the root of the disturbance. And it was Freud who came up with a method to treat it.[64]

Needless to say, Freud's theories were met with open skepticism. Here was a Jewish neurologist from Vienna who claimed that the ills of society were a result of our hidden sexual wishes. Not only was there explicit anti-Semitism that he had to overcome, but the zeitgeist of the time fostered a self-serving view of the individual as moral and self-restrained. Freud emerged in a society that was both ready for him and terrified of him.

Victorian society's fear of inner depravity, so clearly drawn in the characters of Dr. Jekyll and Mr. Hyde, found a real ally in Freud. Not only did Freud scare the bourgeoisie, he also helped give shape to their fears. Over the course of his work, he became an ally with the societal fearfulness, giving aid to the aspect of society that longed to control what was irrational, depraved, and only precariously in their control. Freud gave Europe "scientific" evidence by positing an unconscious, a place where all that we fear about ourselves resides. And, with his method, he assured society that, if they surrendered to his viewpoint, they would gain both health and protection against the onslaught of their destructive impulses.

About this same time in Switzerland, the young psychiatrist Carl Jung was also making a name for himself by developing scientific evidence for the existence of the unconscious. Although he is perhaps best known for his work on personality types, the collective unconscious, and his spiritual views of the Self, Jung began quite pragmatically to scientifically establish a foundation for the existence of "complexes" that operate outside of our awareness. He did this through word association experiments that tracked the length of time it took for a person to respond to a target word. By analyzing the pattern of responses, Jung was able to determine the nature of what was disturbing the person. Applications of this method found their way into the justice system in Switzerland, with Jung quickly gaining fame through his ability to identify criminality and guilt.

For Jung, however, the importance of his work rested more with the instantiation of the unconscious as an influential partner in our conscious lives. In much the same way that Freud asserted the mysterious symptoms of the hysteric were metaphoric manifestations of an inner relationship to sexuality, so Jung was determining that conscious behavior was a result of inner "unconscious disturbances." It didn't take long for them to discover their common ground.

Initially through correspondence, Jung introduced himself to Freud in 1906, and shared some of his writings. Freud responded positively, and soon they became quite close friends and collaborators. Although their relationship only lasted seven years, it altered much of the landscape of Western psychology.[65]

Freud, the elder of the two, took on a fatherly mentor role, and Jung, through the force of his character, became Freud's champion, not only in Switzerland, but in Europe and the United States as well. Jung, unlike Freud, was outgoing and energetic. He also helped diffuse the criticism of psychoanalysis as a "Jewish science" via his Christian background and social standing.

Freud made Jung president of the first psychoanalytic association and editor of the first psychoanalytic journal. To say that Freud loved Jung as a son would be an understatement. For a time, Jung basked in the rays of Freud's brilliance. He was a faithful son who deferred to his father. But soon, like all children, Jung grew up. He had ideas of his own and longed for Freud's approval. Unfortunately, Freud had little interest in broadening his ideas to include the directions that Jung was exploring. In the correspondence of these two ill-fated friends, we see Freud's desperate entreaties for Jung to stay close to the theories of sexuality that Freud valued and protected with his life. And, although we can reasonably imagine that Freud tried to appreciate Jung's ideas, there was something in him that resisted.

Jung perceived a unique value within the unconscious: the strivings of a mind attempting to heal itself. Jung, unlike Freud, worked in a psychiatric hospital. His days were filled, not with the repressed sexuality of the bourgeoisie, but with the seemingly irrational ramblings of patients with dementia praecox, known today as schizophrenia. Jung describes in his autobiography how he began to listen to his patients and wonder whether there was meaning to be found in the paranoia and delusions.[66] In that lurid and magical thinking, he found elements of mythology that he believed were part of a collective heritage of human struggle.

Freud eventually rejected Jung's ideas outright. The pain both men felt from this schism cannot be overstated. For Freud it was a betrayal, and for Jung it was an abandonment. For both it was a rupture that threatened their personal and professional lives. Jung resigned his positions as president of the psychoanalytic association and editor of the journal. In 1913, they exchanged their last letter, which Jung ended with these words, undoubtedly in homage to Hamlet's death scene: "The rest is silence."[67]

Victorian society, as Freud experienced it, suffered due to its repressive relationship to sexuality. In conceptualizing his world in this way, Freud was on reasonably solid ground. Sexuality was certainly repressed in Victorian Europe, and it no doubt was causing physical and psychological problems. But Freud's reluctance to admit other potential causes of human suffering seems to point to a deeper issue.[68]

In my view, the split between Freud and Jung represents a broad fissure in Western society that Freud seemed destined to awkwardly mediate on our behalf. In simple terms, the fissure appears to center on our relationship to our own minds—the non-conscious mind—which Freud viewed with suspicion and Jung with hope.[69]

Today, Freud's model of the mind has limited influence, or so it seems. Most of us analysts and psychotherapists practicing deep psychotherapeutic work no longer rely on Freud's model of healing.

What was called the "metapsychology" of Freud was debunked and dismantled in the 1980s and 90s.[70] His view that sexuality is the root cause of neurosis has certainly faded from prominence. Today, as we have seen in earlier chapters, understandings of attachment, self, emotion, neural functioning, and postmodernism have replaced Freud's reductive understanding of development and treatment. Unfortunately, however, the rejection of Freud has not changed the underlying Fear that Western society seems to experience around the parts of us that we cannot ever fully know or control. Our fear of ourselves—in particular, our fear of our own mind—is still troubling us and shaping our personal and societal experience.

In recent years, the trend in psychotherapy has shifted to what is generally called cognitive behavioral therapy (CBT). This way of working is not heavily dependent upon a model of the mind that includes non-conscious processes or the existence of developmental causes. CBT seeks to remove symptoms by changing conscious thought and behavior. For example, a patient who has a fear of spiders might be asked by a therapist to systematically expose and desensitize themselves with images of spiders and by eventually approaching actual spiders. Although CBT works quite effectively with certain symptoms such as phobias, it is not an approach that takes into consideration the whole of the person. A CBT therapist and patient are no longer required to look into the dark of the mind for answers; the answers are right there in the spoken words and observed actions. To my thinking, CBT and the general shift in the orientation of psychotherapy are less about the real or perceived advantages of one approach over the other, and more about our fear of something within us that we have been running from since long before CBT, or even Freud.

The Dark in the Mind

As we came to see, our non-conscious minds are doing much more in running our lives than we might like to acknowledge. In his book, *The Illusion of Conscious Will*, Daniel M. Wegner paints a compelling argument against our supposed position at the helm of our governance.[71] One of the important points he begins with is that because it "feels" to us like we are initiating our actions, we take this to be the case. Science, however, paints a different picture. The act of willing something, Wegner reveals, is so fraught with complexities and underlying causes that it is almost impossible to clearly identify what is actually taking place when "we" decide to take action—whether that decision is the primary source of the action or merely the secondary response to an order given by our non-conscious minds. Wegner goes on to posit that, because of this nexus of action and response, our sense of willing our actions is at best something of an illusion. Wegner is not alone in this perspective. Going back to William James, there has been profound questioning of our supremacy in relation to our acts of will. Merlin Donald, the cognitive neuroscientist from Case Western University, expresses it this way:

> They have argued that the conscious mind
> gives us the pleasant illusion of control, while
> in reality it can do nothing but stare helplessly
> and stupidly (since it is also inherently shallow)
> at the game of life as it passes by, because all
> our important mental games are played entirely
> unconsciously.[72]

Clearly, we can see that Donald is in the camp that stresses non-conscious processes. But, as he notes, he is not a hardliner. Even though he does refer to us as "cognitive zombies,"[73] he does find value in consciousness. We are not, in his view, merely automatons, but consciousness does create a paradox: it is what we tend to value most and what truly makes us human, but, in point of fact, it is a quite limited function in relation to the whole of our mind. This is what I would like to emphasize. In my view, it is not that consciousness lacks value—it is just infinitesimally small in relation to the vastness of our non-conscious mind.

The recognition of the paradox of consciousness makes us wonder how it is that we fail to recognize these seemingly obvious limitations. To my thinking, our barriers in perceiving our limitations in consciousness stem from the fact that our minds are inherently self-absorbed. To us, the easiest explanation available is that, since we are aware of our thoughts, we must be the one in charge. In this way, it is a bit like the nature of magic and illusion. We perceive an outcome and attribute it to an observed chain of events, ignorant of the underlying, actual causality. Marvin Minsky, in his 1985 book *The Society of Mind*, brings this starkly into focus, saying, "None of us enjoys the thought that what we do depends on processes we do not know; we prefer to attribute our choices to volition, will, or self-control."[74]

In many ways, our fear of not being in control is justified. Not only are our Imaginations continually producing images and working on adaptive solutions, but even simple actions such as deciding to turn our head might possibly be initiated subconsciously. Benjamin Libet, a neurosurgeon, has done a number of studies using brain stimulation to explore this issue. In his studies, he has examined the question of volition by observing the initiation of thought and behavior while measuring neural electrical activation. He discovered that, in simple physical actions such as picking up a glass, our brains are initiating these actions microseconds before we have the thought, "I think I will pick up that glass." This reveals that our sense that we are making choices to initiate physical movements is somewhat inaccurate.[75] Our brains and non-conscious minds seem to be doing much more than we realize. And there is an understandable vulnerability in considering ourselves to be a bit less in control than we like to believe.

As we have seen, so much of our society has emerged to ward off feelings of being less in control. The very fact that we presume more agency than we actually possess may be evidence of our discomfort with our inescapable vulnerability. From the very existence of "courage" across diverse cultures, to the ways in which we build psychological defenses against emotional pain, to the elaborate structures of technology arming us against societal insecurity, we see significant evidence that people don't like being afraid and like admitting it even less.

Returning to my patient Mason from earlier in the chapter, we can see our non-conscious minds are home not only to our rich and vital Imaginations, but also to our pain and suffering. Past experiences, many of which carry unresolved pain, come to rest within us in what is loosely called long-term memory. What makes this particularly problematic is that our security systems, what we are calling Fear, are built to keep us away from danger. One of the primary signals to our brains that we are close to danger is pain. So, if our threat detection systems discover pain within us, they are constitutionally wired to keep us away from that pain.

The ways in which our mind does this are called psychological defenses. These include more benign experiences, such as positive thinking, rationalization, devaluation, contextualization, and avoidance. We all use these defenses to some degree in our daily lives when the pain is not too severe. But defenses such as splitting and dissociation are used by our minds when our pain threatens to overwhelm us. These are the defenses born from trauma, and they happen *to us* and not *with us*. In using the term trauma, it is important to note that we are identifying experience that is overwhelming to the nervous system. This can result from what is called acute trauma, such as abduction, sexual assault, physical assault, or torture, but it can also occur from what is sometimes called "small t" trauma. This lesser form of trauma refers to ongoing experiences that cumulatively come to be too much for the nervous system to manage. Mild forms of neglect, lack of emotional validation, or even too much relentless parental supervision can lead to what we call "small t" traumas. These are the "little too much" or "little too little" disruptions that make it necessary for our minds to take more drastic measures to ensure survival. Figuratively, we build walls, we bury parts of ourselves, or we run. But what is happening inside us is quite problematic. Our minds have the ability to break connections to memory, to partition off what is unwanted, and to split the personality into many pieces. And when these defenses become chronic, it becomes very difficult to restore our well-being.

What is tragic in this equation of Fearing our own minds is that the very experiences within us that most need our care and attention— our pain and suffering—become a threat to us, something that must be defended against. We turn our backs on ourselves and, in the process of staying alive, we lose what is most precious to us— our minds.

Chapter Six

Can You Imagine?

"...the less fear and doubt are embedded in the instructional process, the easier it will be to take the natural steps of learning."

—W. Timothy Gallwey

As a therapist, I am often painfully aware of the inability to reach someone caught in despair. Every attempt to bring light into their darkness fails. The mind of someone in despair is a bit like concrete: nothing gets in; nothing gets out. All efforts to help seem to fail. And even though the hopelessness they are experiencing might not be as dark as they feel it to be, to that person, the despair is real and inescapable.

I saw a young man like this some time ago for a first session. He knew despair and this form of darkness all too well. To him, it felt like someone sitting on his chest, and he couldn't get him off. Little by little, everything in this man's life seemed to have a dusting of gray on it. He would see the future moving farther and farther away while he remained trapped in a painful and disappointing present. He longed to escape but lacked hope that he ever would.

"I can't imagine... I just can't imagine anything ever changing," he kept repeating. "I just can't imagine."

As I sat with this idea, I began to wonder about how often these words show up in my work. More than my interest in the exact words, I wondered about the feeling, the difficulty people have with seeing possibility in the future. For some, like this young man, it was part of a much deeper, all-encompassing depression. But for others, I discovered, it could take shape as a feeling of stuckness in a particular area of their lives, or more subtly, as a vague absence of desire. Regardless of the form it took, not being able to "visualize" the future brought with it a feeling of disappointment, sadness, regret, and at times, emptiness.

I began to realize that the cognitive and emotional movement that brings us from the present to the future is important to our feelings of satisfaction; and equally, as we discovered in Chapter Four, the anxiety-filled movement that brings us experientially from the present to the future is tied to our ability to Imagine.

What Is Imagination?

As a figure of speech, the words, *I can't imagine,* or some version of them, are quite common in everyday language. We all use them occasionally. But for some reason, on that morning, this expression evoked a wondering in me.

In its colloquial sense, "I can't imagine" is a convenient way to convey a subjective experience of improbability, something beyond the norms of what one would expect or want to expect. It may be that a possibility seems ridiculous or painfully impossible, or it may even reveal a sense of impropriety regarding a particular possibility.

Although to imagine is a form of cognition, this type of statement is quite different from saying, "I can't *remember* his name." Although there is some surface similarity in that both types of statement seem to be referring to mental operations (imagining in the former and memory in the latter), the difference is that, as a figure of speech, the former type of statement is not intended to offer an assessment of one's own cognitive capacities. We are not saying, "My imagination is not working right now." Instead, we are referring to what is personally conceivable to us. As an expression, it is more existential than cognitive, more about the scope of one's personal universe and less about how well one's brain is functioning.

The experience of Imagination that we are considering here reflects the sense that beneath the surface of our awareness is a mind that is continually working creatively. Research by the neuroscientist Antonio Damasio supports this. Beneath awareness, our brains are producing images, the favored language of the brain and mind. The production of these images happens, according to Damasio, through the ongoing play of the brain in relation to consciousness.[76] Damasio reasons that this non-conscious part of the mind is so immense that most of the images produced never reach consciousness.

Nancy Andreasen, a professor of psychiatry at Iowa Carver College of Medicine, has done meaningful work in attempting to identify and measure this aspect of the mind. In her book *The Creating Brain: The Neuroscience of Genius*, she attempted to understand the minds of artists who are objectively viewed as geniuses. She discovered in the self-reports of artists, such as the eighteenth-century English poet Samuel Coleridge, an almost exclusive attribution of creative agency to some non-conscious process.

In one example, Coleridge described how the lines of his poem *Kubla Khan* came to him in a dream fully formed as "images [that] rose up before him as things."[77] Upon waking, Coleridge wrote down as much as he could remember, some two hundred-plus lines. He regretfully had to consciously fill in a few blanks.

Andreasen likewise believes that the human brain is a self-organizing system with tremendous complexity and equal potential. The old adage that we use only 10 percent of our brains is perhaps more right than we might imagine.

Damasio adds to this picture with his recognition that the human capacity for conscious creation is what truly sets us apart as a species—and further, that conscious creation only became possible through the evolution of a mental space that our primate relatives significantly lack. Going by many names, this is a space in which images can be held and consciously manipulated. Cognitive scientists such as Stephen Kosslyn refer to this as *reflective space*.[78]

Mark Turner and Gilles Fauconnier call it the space of *conceptual blending*,[79] and Merlin Donald, the neuroscientist, simply identifies it as *consciousness*.[80] It is the space in which we use something we know to understand something we don't. And, as we began to consider in Chapter Four, it is in this space that the seeds of an Imagined future take root.

What I have found in my work is that Imagination is vital to well-being. I am not speaking specifically of the artist, the inventor, or the entrepreneur; I am talking about how each of us is dependent upon the Imagination for our capacity to adapt and to bring forth who we will be in the next moment.

Imagination, as I expressed in Chapter Three, came into existence to see what might be hiding in the dark. And yet, what we find is that Imagination appears not to have limited itself to this narrow purpose. Imagination allowed us not only to see potential danger in the future, but alternatively, it allowed us to *envision ourselves* in a better, safer future.

Imagination gave us the rare capacity to adapt to changing environmental and psychological conditions. No other species appears to be able to adjust, adapt, and survive as well as we do. And, most important to note, much of this process of Imaginative adaptation happens on a non-conscious level. Imagination, it appears, is continually working to adapt and generate new possibilities for an ever-changing future, even without our knowing it.

It is interesting to consider as well that some of these adaptations appear to be related more to satisfaction, meaning, and pleasure than merely to survival. Our minds naturally seek out what "feels good" to us, and we consciously consider possibilities that seem to be *right for us*. Our Imaginations, on both a conscious and non-conscious level, appear to support the unfolding of who we are and who we might become.

In artistic creation, artists may "feel" the seeds of a work forming within them. It may be a color or an image or an emotional tone.

There may be a desire to express a particular pain or a meaning from the human condition. It may be a startling experience of beauty found in nature and a longing to share that beauty. Or it may be a sense of something missing, something to be searched for.

Michelangelo, it is said, spent excessive amounts of time selecting his marble for a sculpture. He did this because he believed that the creation he was envisioning existed within the marble itself and that his work as a craftsman was merely to uncover the creation. In this, we find both the humble recognition of his indebtedness to an a priori source, possibly divine, and equally, a projection of something happening within his own mind. In other words, the metaphorical marble in which Michelangelo found his creations might best be considered the *marble of the mind.*

These qualities of Imagination are recognized by most artists, but I would propose that they are something all of us need to appreciate to a greater degree. Imagination is what happens when we self-actualize. It is the curator in our ongoing desire to express ourselves, and it is what is missing or faulty when we have difficulty seeing ourselves in the future.

Although it does appear that Imagination emerged to help Fear promote security, this was not the end of the road for Imagination. From there, our minds continued to evolve ever greater capacities for invention, creativity, and meaning. Little of this had to do with the need for safety. Fear may have planted the first seeds, but Imagination continued to cross-pollinate in ways that seem to go against the original imperative of security. Imagination, in its self-fulfilling role, puts us at risk. Curiosity did kill the cat, and Fear remembers. The oppression of Imagination by Fear was unavoidable in the pursuit of survival. If bringing forth who we are threatens our existence, then what other choice does Fear have but to shut it down?

Imagination is self-organizing and seems to enjoy the playful invention of self. Without this, we find ourselves limited in our ability to move into the future, to find hope, and to engage meaningfully with life. It is not just a loss of creativity or an inability to make our lives more interesting. Imagination is the platform that transforms mere existence into meaning.

This is a fight we have been fighting for as long as we have had consciousness. Fear strives for security, and Imagination strives for meaning. And as we will see, it is not just our individual lives today that are touched by this struggle. The very history of Western culture has been shaped by it.

The Day We Lost the Fight

For more than one thousand years, following the fall of Rome, Fear held our Imaginations captive. It began around 400 AD and lasted into the Renaissance, and even beyond. The imprisonment of our minds was achieved through a form of religious doctrine enacted by a bishop who gained influence in the early Catholic Church through his writings on human weakness, particularly his own. This was Augustine of Hippo, known to most of us theologically and philosophically as St. Augustine.

The time in which Augustine was promoting these ideas coincided with the rise of Christianity. Rome officially adopted Christianity in 380 AD, and, over the course of the next several hundred years, its influence spread across Europe, into the Middle East, and down into Northern Africa. This was, according to some historians, a very precarious time in which barely 5 percent of the population was anything other than a slave or a peasant. Invasions by barbarians and Goths, widespread disease, and changing social, political, and religious structures all undoubtedly made this a time of tremendous upheaval. Yet Christianity seemed to thrive in "the ruins of Rome."[81]

As part of this societal movement, Augustine was able to imprison the mind by legislating against "curiosity," which he viewed as a threat. In fact, starting in about 400 AD, Augustine explicitly designated curiosity a sin.

In his writings on curiosity, several themes emerge. All of them, however, seem to pivot on the basic idea that curiosity leads human beings away from the contemplative, and thus away from God. Augustine called curiosity a "disease,"[82] and associated it with a "lust of the eyes."[83] He considered human beings lowly creatures who were vulnerable to temptations of the flesh. The eyes, being of the flesh, could be caught by curious sights that were strange and beautiful. While at home in contemplation of God, Augustine grieved the ways in which even his own mind could be diverted by the curious sight of "lizards catching flies."[84] Eyes were the "princes of the senses"[85] and as such should be directed only to the divine.

To the Church at this time, the only sight worthy of the eyes was the Bible. Other books came to represent a knowledge that took us away from God. Augustine promoted this association of curiosity with forbidden knowledge. There were, according to him, realms of knowledge that were inappropriate for us mortals to explore. These included the morbid, the grotesque, the dark arts, astrology, and divination. These were often called the "curious arts."[86] But more than this, any pursuit of knowledge for its own sake was viewed as sinful. As lowly creatures within the early Christian cosmology, it was seen as morally inappropriate for us to ask too many questions. The most iconic example of this is the story of the fall in the Garden of Eden.

This time witnessed a marked decline in intellectual pursuits. Libraries were destroyed and texts were burned. Many philosophers and educators fled to Persia in the East, taking with them as much of their intellectual heritage as they could carry. Some of this destruction of knowledge happened at the hands of the Goths, who were out to destroy the existing culture, but this cannot adequately explain the comprehensive retreat from knowledge.

By 529 AD, Justinian, the Emperor of Rome, officially closed the Academy in Athens. Education was limited to the religious, as were virtually all texts written at this time.[87] Book production dropped dramatically while the Church was gaining power through the assimilation of pagan culture. Knowledge, unfortunately, was linked to the pagan. The many gods of Greece and Rome became the one God; a God that Augustine claimed didn't want us to know too much.

Although Augustine's views on the sinfulness of curiosity were highly influential in the evolution of Western culture,[88] it would be an overstatement to attribute the vast changes in our relationship to knowledge, culture, and the mind solely to the effects of his writings. Much was changing societally and culturally leading up to that moment, and not all of it was visible. Augustine's pronouncement on curiosity may have merely ridden the wave of change already in motion. Something was shifting in the very fabric of society. And even though we can view these new societal constraints through many lenses, from a psychological perspective, what happened following the decline of Rome was a critical moment in the evolution of Imagination.

In many ways, the devastation during the Middle Ages is not so different from what happens to all of us at times within our own minds. Augustine and the Church struggled to confine the natural urges of curiosity and desire, and ultimately, the mind itself. They justified this confinement with religious law—a fear-based law that was intended to bring us closer to God and to avoid the risk of damnation that followed sinfulness. This fear-based confinement was meant for our own good; *limit curiosity, limit desire, keep the mind small.* But as we see in our own lives, the cost of safety can be quite high—the ideas we never follow, the feelings we never express, and sadly, the person we never become.

What we now need to explore more fully is what makes us as human beings so vulnerable to Fear. What happened along the way to our becoming human that promoted such a state? And why is it that other animals don't have these problems?

Natal Inferiority

I will never forget the cat I took off the street in Hell's Kitchen, in New York City. She was feral, and I was surprised that the rescue crew was able to catch her. I found out why a few days later when the vet told me she was going to have kittens. Within weeks, I was the proud father of six adorable kittens who very quickly learned to run as a pack full speed down the length of my tiny railroad apartment.

What stands out most to me about that experience is the lengths to which the mother cat went to care for her kittens. Coming to know her as I did, I saw that she was still wild, fiercely independent, and always cautious about human interaction. I remember the first time I tried to pick her up. At first she was very still, and then, once I got her up into my arms, she began to flail her limbs with claws extended, slashing my arms, chest, neck, and face. The fact that this feral and possibly traumatized cat allowed herself to be captured and put into a cage awaiting adoption was, to my mind, a selfless act of submission driven by the maternal imperative to find a safe place to deliver her kittens.

Giving birth was no different. From the moment I saw a sac emerge at two in the morning, she was a birthing machine. She assiduously opened each sac, cleaned the kitten, ate the sac, and then rested, panting, until the next kitten emerged. After five of these deliveries, she was clearly exhausted. I thought she was done. It didn't seem possible that she could do any more, but then one more sac emerged. And before she allowed herself to rest, all six kittens were cleaned and nestled up to the soft warmth of her belly.

After that, she refused to leave her nest in my closet for two days. I brought her food, but she didn't eat. Evidently, the protein from the sacs was sufficient nutrition to get her through this initial period in which she protected her newborns following delivery. And in the day-to-day care that followed, she was present, efficient, and seemingly free of her own needs.

In contrast, the second thing that stands out in my memory of her is the subtle process by which she began to separate from her kittens. On the surface, this almost looked like boredom, or lack of maternal care. As the weeks passed and the kittens began to eat on their own, she would feed them less meticulously. Almost without rhyme or reason, she would sometimes randomly get up and walk away from them. This is not to say that she lost warmth in her mothering, but she was more selective in her giving of it. At night, mother and kittens would still lie together all in one big fur ball, but during the day, she might leave them and do her own thing. Her mothering was remarkably unencumbered, and it allowed her kittens to mature and play freely. She had brought them to near self-sufficiency, and she was allowing them to fend for themselves. But more than this, she intuitively knew when it was time to set them free.

For us human beings, it is a bit different. Rather than a mother staying committed and attached for two short months, we need our mothers and/or fathers to stay vigilantly connected and attentive for many years.[89] Human babies, more than any other species, come into the world with a profound natal inferiority. We are helpless for much longer than other animals. And without the capacity of our caregivers to remain connected and caring for this extended period of time, none of us would have survived.

How Big Is Too Big?

The evolution of our brain is very much tied to the question of when we first can be called human.[90] *Homo habilis* is believed to be the first species with rudimentary language. Does this warrant the status of first human? From the fossil record, we can determine that the brain of *Homo habilis* three million years ago was approximately six hundred cubic centimeters. This brain size is close to what we find today with chimpanzees. But from that point in our evolution, brain size increases dramatically. About a million years after *Homo habilis*, *Homo erectus* possessed a brain almost twice as large. What is striking in this development is that this increase in brain volume takes place without a commensurate increase in body size. *Homo sapiens'* brain today is about 1,400 cubic centimeters, and much of this expansion occurred in the last five hundred thousand years. Also of note is that the paleocortex, the older cortical brain, is virtually the same for us as it is for many other mammals. What increases so dramatically for us is what is called the neocortex. That's the good stuff.

Paralleling this development in brain size was the already-mentioned shift toward bipedalism. *Homo ergaster/erectus* walked in an increasingly upright manner, and this shift required some changes in our biomechanics. Principal among these changes was the narrowing of the pelvis and lengthening of the legs. This facilitated walking upright for longer distances and allowed for greater migratory possibilities. What emerged from these shifts, however, is what is sometimes called a *pelvic constraint*. How do you birth a big-headed baby and keep it alive long enough for its big brain to develop?

This problem was solved by extending intrauterine brain development over a longer period of time. Gestation across species is linked directly to brain size, from twenty-one days for the rat to 165 days for the macaque monkey to 280 days for the human being.[91] But even this extension appears to have not quite done the trick. A chimpanzee's brain at birth is about 45 percent of its eventual adult brain size. The macaque monkey's brain at birth is 70 percent of adult size, but woefully, the human infant is born with a brain that is just 25 percent of adult brain volume. And what we then discover is that, during the first year of life, the chimpanzee acquires 85 percent of its adult brain size. The human infant will require approximately six full years to reach this same 85 percent of its adult brain capacity. The implications of this neurodevelopmental need cannot be overstated.

Because our brains got bigger and our pelvises got smaller, the solution required a postnatal process that would allow our brains to develop outside the womb. Without the natural protection of the womb, how then were we to keep the newborn alive long enough to reach an independent viability?

Given the vulnerability of the human infant at birth, as well as the years required for that child to be able to manage their own security, evolution required something creative. Building on the basic primate systems for maternal care, humans developed a neuro/psycho/physiological system that would keep mother and child locked together. This system, as noted earlier, is called "attachment," and it is what keeps a child connected to a caregiver long enough to reach a relative state of autonomy.[92]

In essence, this attachment system of relational connection monitors and maintains an optimal proximity between caregiver and child. When the distance becomes too great, the infant and/or child experiences distress. This is part of the alarm system we talked about in Chapter Two that activates anxiety, fear, and panic. The cries of an insecure infant alert the mother to close the distance between them and to soothe. With age and maturity, the tolerable distance for the child increases until, eventually, the child becomes able to exist securely and separate from the caregiver. This presents another unique challenge for both mother and child, negotiating the need for closeness and equally the need for freedom.

I have watched my wife meet this delicate balance with our son. Quite simply and beautifully, she expresses the work of a mother as "needing to figure out just how much to let go every day." Not an easy task. She does it well.

In the earliest stages of this negotiation, infant security is maintained through both tactile and visual means. Much research and theory has gone into understanding the ways in which the gaze between mother and infant aids in emotional regulation and the furthering of security. Eleanor Gibson and Richard Walk, working together at Cornell University in 1960, devised an ingenious experiment to look at how juvenile animals and human infants use their mothers to negotiate depth and the dangers of height.[93] The experiment came to be known as the Visual Cliff. Taken up later by James Sorce and Robert Emde, the experiment eventually began to look not just at how juvenile animals come to learn the dangers of height, but ultimately, how infants use maternal signaling to learn what is safe and what isn't.[94]

The experimental situation consisted of a platform half of which was covered with checkerboard tiles. At the midpoint, the tiles changed to clear plexiglass. Through the plexiglass could be observed a drop of three feet to a floor that again had checkerboard linoleum tiles. The infant was placed on the checkerboard end of the platform and given toys to play with. After a few minutes, the toys were moved to the far end of the platform, where there was clear plexiglass. The mother was also at the far end of the platform. The infants, wanting to get to the toys, would start to crawl toward the toys and thus toward the clear plexiglass. Invariably, when the infants reached the plexiglass, they would freeze, evidently confused and unsure of their footing. What is most notable, however, is that when faced with this uncertainty or ambiguity, the infants looked to their mothers' faces. Prior to the experiment, the mothers were assigned to one of two groups. The first group was given instructions to have an encouraging look on their faces, and the second group was instructed to appear fearful (or angry).

The results of the experiment revealed that, when the mothers had encouraging and relaxed expressions, the babies resumed crawling and reached the toys. But when the babies looked up and saw fearful expressions on their mothers' faces, they froze and would not proceed. These results, which have been replicated repeatedly, indicate that infants at about ten months of age are using their mothers' facial expressions to guide their actions. But more than this, we see how our inclinations for curiosity and exploration can be directly shaped by social determinations of what is safe.

The fact that we are hardwired to be sensitive to what is going on in the face of a caregiver may not be a surprise. I think we have all experienced the ways in which a well-timed look from our mothers can seemingly stop us in our tracks. Perhaps more important to us here is the awareness that this system of restriction is far more ubiquitous than we might have previously imagined.

The messages we receive as infants and children about what is safe and what isn't are both explicit and implicit. They are coming at us in a continual stream of permission and restriction, looks of encouragement and discouragement—how we eat, how we play, how we sleep, how we walk, how we run, how we study, how we use the bathroom, how we deal with illness.

These messages are all shaped by the subjectivity of our parents, our communities, and our societies. Unfortunately, the cumulative effects of these subjective restrictions not only alter our behavioral freedom to follow our interests, but they also affect the very fabric of our selves and minds.

The limitations on exploration and play that fear produces in mammals are particularly problematic for human beings. Our brains and minds evolved into self-organizing systems that are less like a computer and more like a playground. Much as with the role of play that we explored in Chapter One, here we can say that play is the work of a healthy mind; and further, that a healthy mind is the foundation for a healthy self. This is what D. W. Winnicott, one of the early psychoanalytic pioneers in infant and child development, meant when he said, "It is in playing and only in playing that the individual child or adult is able to be creative and to use the whole personality. And it is only in being creative that the individual discovers the self."[95]

Injecting overwhelming or chronic relational Fear into a child's life not only inhibits their play activities, it literally inhibits the playful functioning of their Imagination, and in turn, their ability to be who they might become.[96]

For much of her life, Robin considered herself a people-pleaser, someone who liked to be liked and worked hard to be a good friend and eventually, a good partner in marriage. Her husband had been in therapy before, but Robin had never done any work on herself. Her husband suggested she go into therapy to work on her explosive anger that came out when they argued. The way Robin described it was that everything would be fine, and then all of a sudden, "it would all come out." And unfortunately, the words she used weren't just angry, they were mean.

Our initial work centered on helping Robin to become more in touch with her feelings, to notice the tiny moments of emotion, sensation, and feeling. This work proved valuable to her, and she felt hopeful. But as we began to look beneath the surface, Robin realized that she had no idea who she was. She didn't know what her favorite movies were, what music she liked, or even why she had come to live in New York City.

With this emerging reality, we wondered together about where those feeling states of individuality were, why they were not known to her, and whether they even existed at all. Small moments of unacknowledged disappointment and emotional hurt led us to realize that she was missing important aspects of who she was. She wasn't sure if she was dismissing them, rationalizing them away, or just not noticing them. But regardless, they were not available to her.

With time, as Robin began to check in more with her inner experience, she described the feeling of walking on eggshells with her husband. It was subtle, she told me, not so obvious—to her or to anyone else. She described a sensitivity she had to the needs of her husband, and to others more generally. She prided herself on being able to meet those needs. This could take the form of thoughtful actions, such as remembering to pick up her husband's favorite cereal or sending a thank-you card to his mother. But in many ways, we discovered this "eggshell" experience was primarily an attempt to attune to her husband's emotional state. She said that he wasn't always so easy to read and that she considered herself pretty good at reading emotions, but not always his.

What began to unfold, in the work between us, was a growing awareness that somehow the "good childhood" she remembered was also a childhood in which she experienced a significant degree of restrictive fear. In her early childhood, she remembered that she had trouble sleeping alone and would often wake her mother for comfort. Her mother was reassuring and would sit with her daughter in her bed till she fell asleep. Robin also remembered having fears of burglars breaking into the house and kidnapping her. She worried about getting lost when they traveled and wanted to hold hands with her mom in public spaces up until she was at least twelve years old.

As we explored the nature of these memories one day, Robin had an image of her mother's face come to mind. When I asked her to describe it, she had some difficulty. She could see the hair and the outline of the face quite clearly, but the eyes, mouth, and facial expression were all out of focus. Was her mother happy, sad, angry, frightened? For some reason, Robin had difficulty identifying the emotional state of her mother in that image. And as we sat with this experience, Robin began to cry. "I don't know what she's feeling. What is she feeling? What are you feeling?!" she yelled in desperation.

Little by little, Robin came to remember that much of her early life was spent unconsciously trying to figure out what her mother was feeling. She and I began to piece together the sense that, in those early years, her mother was undoubtedly depressed. Not only was she hard to read, but often what was on her face was frightening to Robin. Parental depression can have significant impact upon a child's sense of security. The inability to reach a depressed parent emotionally evokes a feeling of uncertainty and unpredictability. Not only was Robin's mother inscrutable, her depression made meaningful connection difficult for her. This undermined the very systems that might have helped Robin know how to respond, when to be afraid and when to relax. Instead, Robin was reduced to a relentless hypervigilance, desperately attempting to read her mother and wondering how to reconcile the experience of her mother as both present and abandoning in the same moment. And all the while, Robin hid her feelings of fear from herself and her family beneath the persona of a "good girl." This disguise made it easier for her to remain positively attached to her caregivers.

So dominating was this pursuit that anything that even remotely interfered with this vigilance needed to be eradicated. On an unconscious level, the parts of Robin that needed security had figured out an adaptation to her problem. She needed to eliminate anything that might distract her from the vigilance required. What appears to have been most distracting to her, what interfered most directly, were her own individual needs and desires. It is as if her mind slowly began to turn down the volume on these internal longings until eventually she stopped noticing them. Without awareness of these, Robin remained stuck in a form of unhealthy attunement to her mother.

We might say that the anger which eventually burst through for her was a form of health—a reestablishing of her right to have her needs and desires. And while this conception makes sense, it didn't work so well for her in reality. So strong was her form of psychological captivity that following the anger outbursts, Robin would become flooded with guilt and shame, and retreat back to the security of her padded cell, locking the door with her own key.

From this example with Robin, we glimpse several aspects of difficulty that emerge in the relationship between Fear and Imagination. Most broadly, we see the central flaw in human security. Human security is dependent upon an attachment system that is at best subjective and at worst prone to distortion. The life experiences of the caregiver shape the subjectivity of threat assessment, and this not only guides parenting but also becomes internalized as part of the infant and child.

The subjectivity in threat assessment has been useful to us as a species in that our security in infancy and childhood does not solely rest upon our innate fears, but also relies upon previous experiences of fear learned by our protectors. Our species survived because we were able to adapt, an adaptation built upon a flexibility in assessing how to survive. But unfortunately, this same flexibility in threat assessment is vulnerable to becoming distorted by a caregiver's traumatic life experience.

Take, for example, the experience of parents holding their children's hands while crossing a street. How different would it be for a parent, and ultimately for their child, if that parent had previously witnessed a child being hit by a car? Even though we all know that children every day are hit by cars, our grip on our child's hand would be inestimably tighter if we had personally suffered such a trauma.

Trauma shapes us in profound ways, most notably around Fear. And what we often find is that the effects spread across domains. In other words, the parent who witnessed a child being hit by a car might not only be hyper-controlling while crossing streets, but also be hyper-controlling in life, in general.

In this, we see another difficult aspect in the connection between Fear and Imagination—the relational lengths we will go to maintain security. And if our security is tied to relational harmony with our primary attachment figures, then our vulnerability to those relationships becomes quite high. For many, like Robin, this brings with it an impossible task: maintain harmony in attachment while furthering personal fulfillment. This is where Imagination becomes most vulnerable.

Because our sense of security has roots in developmental experience, what we go through in infancy, childhood, and adolescence not only directly contributes to our learning about danger, it also directly contributes to who we eventually become. Psychological security is fundamental to a sense of self. If during childhood we were insufficiently supervised, neglected, or abandoned, we might never have fully internalized a balanced sense of attachment, what is called "secure attachment." And without this, we remain in a continual state of attempting to restore what was missing. The problem with this is that Fear changes everything it touches. Our unresolved insecurities drive us to tighten our grip on life, to the point where we literally choke the very breath out of life. We might be able to keep our child from being hit by a car, but if in the process we corrode our child's sense of freedom and Imagination, what have we actually gained? And as we saw with Robin, Fear can demand of us a form of submission in which we must sacrifice our Imagination and our vitality on the altar of survival.

Sadly, a human being can remain in such a state of deprivation for his or her entire life. Meaning and fulfillment are lost; curiosity and Imagination barely function. How many of us live with subtle forms of this? But what we now need to wonder about is what happens to Imagination when it is psychologically marginalized in this way. Is it lost to us? Is it damaged? Can we ever find it again? And if so, what healing does it require?

Chapter Seven

Imaginative Revolution

"Science was destined to remake the world, but in its early days it inspired laughter more often than reverence."

—Edward Dolnick

In the previous chapter, we looked at the oppressive nature of Fear both personally and societally. We saw the ways in which discomfort with curiosity, and ultimately with Imagination, led our minds during the Middle Ages to shut down. And, while it is certainly true that this was a result of restrictions on education and publishing, there appears to be more to it. Our minds collectively submitted to the forces of Fear. But as we know from where we stand today, this darkness did not last forever; something eventually did shift for us as a civilization.

This change might seem to have been inevitable, that the oppression of the Middle Ages quite naturally would have come to an end. I say this because much of what drives us as a society rests upon a bias that growth is endemic to our species. Science, culture, medicine, and even the randomness of evolution seem to operate from an unwritten law that progress marches forward from less to more, from bad to good, from low to high, and from dark to light. Our desperate need to believe in growth is so woven into the fabric of who we are that it is difficult to see that Fear is unquestionably driving the bus.

In his book *Throwing Rocks at the Google Bus*, Douglas Rushkoff supports this notion with a caution about our compulsion toward economic growth and its potential for catastrophe. In his most recent work, *Team Human,* he goes further to say that these blind propensities are not only impacting us economically, but might be threatening our very humanity.[97] I would add to Rushkoff's warning that, even though we as a society believe Imagination has triumphed in the form of progress, the reality is not so simple.

The forces of Fear that brought about societal collapse after Augustine have not disappeared. Imagination may have broken free, but a look at our history makes clear that Fear is still at work.

For a number of my patients, looking back at their developmental histories seems like a waste of time. As one recently described it, "I have so much trouble with the present, why should I bother with the past?" While I do understand the importance of dealing with the present, it is often difficulties with the present that require us to look back in time. For each of us, events during early development necessitate a need to adapt, and sometimes these adaptations send us on life trajectories that don't end up working for us in the long run. For instance, if I mention to a patient that they seem to exclusively favor self-reliance and are unable to ask for help, and wonder with them how this tendency came to develop, they will say something like, "I've been this way for as long as I can remember." Now, it is true that each of us might have come into the world with temperamental differences in this regard, but most likely, an inability to ask for help would be the result of early experiences in which asking for help was less than successful. Looking back at our developmental histories can help us identify what we needed to do to survive, and figure out the long-term cost of these adaptations.

It is the same with us here in this book. In my view, examining the historical cycle that was enacted between Fear and Imagination five hundred years ago gives us an opportunity to understand, not only what shaped us as a species, but how we might readjust today to keep the dysfunctional patterns from repeating. I would argue that the history of Fear and Imagination is anything but dead. Fear and Imagination continue to do battle within each of us, and they continue to shape our society. For this reason, I would like to take a deeper look at what happened to move us out of the Dark Ages and tip the balance back toward Imagination.

Humanity Then

It is difficult to imagine what life was like as we emerged from the Dark Ages. It was a time in which no one bathed, human excrement piled up in gutters, accused witches were executed by the hundreds,[98] and the London Fire and Plagues of 1665 and 1666 were taken as evidence of God's displeasure.[99]

So little of nature was understood that fantastical ideas filled in the blanks at every opportunity. The animation of life, the movements of matter, the workings of the body, all were understood through what today would be called superstition. Rene Descartes himself is reported to have believed that the guilt of a murderer could be determined by bringing him into close proximity to the victim. When this was done, so Descartes believed, the victim's wounds would gush blood anew, thus proving guilt.[100]

Life for the newly emerging artisan class in the 1600s, what we might call the middle class today, although a step up, still provided little opportunity for mobility. Everyone knew their place. Tradespeople learned their craft through apprenticeship or through work in a family trade. There was no need for formal education. Reading and writing were not necessary for most people, certainly not for the masses of peasants and wandering laborers. The first paper mill opened in England in 1600, and printed material was almost nonexistent.

In the cosmology of the seventeenth century, the earth and human beings were understood to be just about as far from heaven as you can get. And even though the earth was thought to be at the center of the universe, such a distinction did not carry honor with it. It was, perhaps, a bit like an alcoholic patient of mine who described himself by saying, "I am the piece of excrement at the center of the universe." This lowly place we held at that time, the still center of the cosmos, was reinforced not only by the Bible, but also by the filth and depravity in which we lived.[101]

What Changed?

The change that eventually transformed the Dark Ages into the Age of Enlightenment is tied most notably to events in the seventeenth century. As a cluster, these events are referred to as the Scientific Revolution, and Isaac Newton is thought to be the father of this transformation. This was a period in which great discoveries in mathematics, astronomy, and the life sciences brought us to a new, more accurate and rational understanding of ourselves and the universe. The invention of new lenses allowed us to see the life hidden in a drop of water and to extend our vision out into space. We discovered the intricacies of anatomy and learned that the earth was not the center of the universe. Newton was able to uncover the nature of light and color, to invent the calculus, and to give us the foundational laws that govern all existence. He "mathematized the world."[102] Without a doubt, we can see from this that Imagination found a way to break free of its prior confinement.

Long before Newton came on the scene, however, a group of men in the early 1600s were laying the foundation for his work. They approached the monarchy of Charles II with a request. They wanted to form a society for the advancement of knowledge, and they wanted the king's blessing. They would call it the Royal Society.

Needless to say, the inception of the Royal Society went unnoticed by all but a few. Those who attended the meetings were members of an elite upper class that came to enjoy the oddities and wonders that were paraded before them. As noted by historians of this period, the initial experiments of the Royal Society were often nothing more than displays of nature's deformities or demonstrations of barbaric torture.[103] Animals were cut open without anesthesia, their lungs inflated with bellows. Transfusions were done between unrelated species of animals. Poisons were given to cats and dogs while onlookers marveled. Newly invented vacuum chambers suffocated dogs and cats, and all varieties of the grotesque were studied beneath the lenses of the newly invented microscope.[104] In one entry of his diary, Samuel Pepys, a frequent visitor and eventual president of the Royal Society, reported somewhat gleefully, "I also saw an abortive child preserved in spirits of salts."[105]

The Royal Society was indeed a strange mix of entertainment, science, and sadistic pleasure. The fact that its work had touches of a sideshow is not surprising. The Middle Ages out of which it grew regularly hosted public executions, punishments, and dissections. It would be wrong to suggest that the inception of the Royal Society brought with it an instantaneous change in the societal mind of the seventeenth century.

As I've argued earlier, societal change is dependent upon the collective psychological state of the individuals that make up that society. Although Newton gets the credit for the big discoveries, and the Royal Society the credit for providing him a platform, it is someone far less known who managed to shift, ever so slightly, the mind's right to wonder.

Sir Francis Bacon was born into the aristocracy in the middle of the sixteenth century and received formal education up through his time at Trinity College at the University of Cambridge. He became first counselor to Queen Elizabeth in 1597 and was influential in much of political life at that time. Bacon also began to question the validity of the imposed limitations on science. He believed that empiricism had much to offer society and its prohibition was holding us back from improving the world. Bacon, it seems, had found a way to imagine.

Specifically, Bacon laid out a new plan for our relationship to nature and to experimentation. He refuted the many criticisms against learning, such as that it invited sloth or made people uncivilized, immoral, or unlawful. He offered us a new vision, not just of science, but of our relationship to knowledge. The prohibitions against learning, the caution around hubris, he believed, were unnecessary and inaccurate.

While Bacon held to the notion that all of science was a demonstration of our love of God, unlike Augustine, he rejected the idea that, because of our devotion to God, we needed to stay ignorant. This was demonstrated in his 1620 work where he quoted Proverbs: "It is the glory of God to conceal a thing, but the glory of a king to search it out."[106] The historian Peter Harrison has questioned whether we can reasonably believe that Bacon was sincere in his reverence for God in relation to science.[107] Of course, it is difficult to answer this question. But, regardless, Bacon was able to avoid a direct assault on the Church, the Bible, or Augustine. Rather than defend the sinful nature of curiosity, Bacon brilliantly pivoted the argument and offered an alternative to curiosity as the originating motivation for science. Charity, he suggested, and not curiosity, should motivate the desire for knowledge and scientific innovation. By charity, he meant a recognition that the fruits of scientific endeavors would benefit God's creatures and that to pursue science was to pursue God's work. He said, let scientists be "like bees, which extract the goodness from nature and use it to make useful things."[108]

Bacon ushered in an optimism through an approach built upon experimentation and documentation. The motto for science would change, he proposed, from *ne plus ultra*, no further, to *plus ultra*, further yet.[109] With an imaginative bravura, he said, "Thus we cannot conceive of any end of external boundary of the world…there must be something beyond."[110]

Through his invitation to experiment and innovate, Bacon was opening the way for people of the seventeenth century to think more for themselves and of themselves. And what is most important for us to understand in this is that Bacon began to elevate the potential of the human being.

To my mind, Bacon was like a societal therapist. He held a vision of change long before his patient could. Like Bacon, as therapists, we help to recognize what the psychoanalyst James Fosshage and others have called the "forward edge" of the patient.[111] This is the place where the natural development of the patient is taking them. This is what Bacon helped do for the seventeenth century. Not only did he caution against accepting outdated philosophical foundations for knowledge, he affirmed that the human being, although ignorant and covered in filth, had value. The imagination, he told his peers, was excited by "that which strikes and enters the mind at once and suddenly."[112] Beneath the superficial filth, Bacon saw the beauty of a mind capable of Imagining. He pulled us out of the filth and dried our soggy brains.

Imagination, as Bacon realized, is profoundly involved in the experience of self and self-worth. But more than this, his plan for freeing Imagination placed human beings in a new relationship to nature and to light. Nature, Bacon believed, was ours for the taking and could be rightfully mastered "by the mind, which is a kind of divine fire."[113] And all the while, Bacon proposed that the work of the scientist was "not for gold, silver, or jewels…but only for God's first creature, which was light. To have light, I say, of the growth of all parts of the world."[114] While Bacon fought back against the ascription of unworthiness through his allegiance to light, God's first creature, we will see in the next chapter how this dynamic reveals his own vulnerability to Fear. Bacon's devotion to the light was equally a declaration of our independence and a manifesto of our insecurity.

Chapter Eight

The Fear Paradox

*"The trouble is, if you don't risk anything, you
risk even more."*

—Erica Jong

Marianne Williamson, the New Age spiritual author, wrote, "It is our light, not our darkness, that most frightens us."[115] Notably, this quote is often falsely attributed to Nelson Mandela. I say notably since Mandela is so firmly linked to the world's fight for freedom, and light, as we have seen, is metaphorically integral to this fight.

The quote from Marianne Williamson is a favorite of mine, but not, perhaps, for the reasons you might imagine. Although I cannot say with certainty what she intended, my sense is that Williamson was attempting to communicate that we as human beings suffer with an unfounded fear of our own unique magnificence. She is communicating her belief that light as a power within us is not to be feared, that false modesty is no substitute for an authentic right to be ourselves. And, finally, that letting our light shine is more than a right, it is an obligation.

Like Williamson's words, freeing our minds from the limitations of Fear is central to what we have been exploring in this book. The societal oppression of curiosity and knowledge after the fall of Rome became a way in which the dark triumphed over the light; and then, after a thousand years of darkness, the Imaginative light and knowledge of the Scientific Revolution broke free. So far, so good.

My interest in Williamson's words here, however, stems from what I see as a potential blind spot for us. For while she is accurate that so many of us suffer needlessly with a dimming of our personal light, there is an unseen and paradoxical danger arising from too much light. What we need to explore further here is that even the gentle warmth of the sun can eventually burn us.

Earlier in the book, I showed that Imagination grew up under the tutelage of Fear. The need to see into the dark, to predict and prepare, was the first task Imagination learned. From there, Imagination appears to have assisted Fear with countless innovations for threat detection, defense, and attack. From the telescope to the CT scan, from the bow and arrow to the atomic bomb, so much of what our civilization has invented is focused on promoting security. Indeed, much of civilization itself could be said to have been born from this union of Fear and Imagination—a union, not inconsequentially, consummated in the dark. In other words, Imagination bears the imprint of Fear from its origins.

But when Imagination was given the task of solving the dark, something unintended happened. The essential qualities of the dark—its uncertainty and unknowability—became, not only the veils that hid danger, but new forms of danger in and of themselves. Tangible fear of what might exist within the dark was generalized into a metaphoric fear of all that was uncontrollable, unknowable and, ultimately, imperfect. This metaphoric experience, arising from our fear of the dark, transformed an understandable desire to stay safe into a paradoxical escalation of danger.

With this in mind, let's take a closer look at how this came about.

Blindness

From my clinical work and studies, I have found that there are two elements at play in our personal and societal attempts to deal with the dark. The first I call the "curation of light" and the second, the "eradication of the dark." And while it will be useful to deal with them here somewhat discretely, in actuality, they are two parts of a whole.

Curating the light is a seemingly benign approach that seeks to neutralize the danger of the dark and quell our insecurity by Imagining that if we "light enough candles"—i.e., become smart enough, rich enough, technologically advanced enough—we can eventually change the dark's very composition.

Eradicating the dark is a more aggressive strategy designed to root out unseen dangers. Much of this work is quite positive in nature, such as our efforts to wipe out unseen killers like cancer, cholera, and the plague. Without a doubt, this eradication has furthered our feelings of security, but it has also brought forth the destructive development of new and better ways to torture, extract confessions, invade online privacy, and exorcise spiritual demons. We might even say that it is present in rituals such as the "laying on of hands" for medical healing and the hope many find in ridding a newborn baby of sin through "baptism." Eradicating the dark has both furthered our security and diminished our humanity.

Paralleling this movement of eradication are the efforts we make to usher in more light. As we saw in the previous chapter, much of this curation is brought about through the expansion of knowledge. Our desire to have the light of knowledge transform the dark has driven us to dissect, categorize, and explain the workings of the natural world. We seek out the how, why, when, and where of cause and effect.

Technological innovation is also prominent in our work to bring greater light to the world. So much of what we invent shows the influence of our longing to be soothed by the light of progress. Many of these innovations shape light within our society in literal ways, such as the use of flint for fire-starting, whale blubber for oil lamps, the invention of the incandescent light bulb, and now, the everlasting LED.

Technology has also attempted to metaphorically satisfy our need for light with inventions such as GPS, heart and activity monitors, laparoscopic surgery, the printing press, space travel, the personal computer, the iPhone, and vision-correcting lenses. We strive to see better, express ourselves more expansively, and extend the reach of our minds to the very edges of the universe. The odyssey of Edison and his ten thousand attempts to find the right filament for the light bulb provides us with a perfect hero in this mythological journey of bringing light to soothe our fearful hearts.

What we fail to see in all these efforts, however, is the intoxication that comes as we follow the light and vanquish the dark. This is the intoxication of righteousness, and it promotes a great deal of the ill effects of the Fear Paradox.

For us personally, the light of righteousness takes shape most precariously through the pursuit of perfection. Dieting, nutritional supplements, helicopter parenting, fashion trends, tutors for college essays, self-help books, personal trainers, cosmetic surgery, and religious dictates on goodness and sin are all ways in which we strive to be perfect. Much of this, I believe, happens unconsciously, and is hidden in the light of good intentions. And because perfection is impossible, the only satisfaction we can extract is the belief that what we do is right.

In my view, the infusion of righteousness into our relationship to light stems from light's age-old connection to security. The value of security was so high for us and light was so integral to it, it is no wonder our pursuit of light has taken on the mantle of "the good." Unfortunately, as we seek to increase light and safety, we simultaneously fill ourselves with an inflating sense of our own virtue. And this is when people get hurt.

In 1945, the Scottish physician and scientist Alexander Fleming gave a speech. He was addressing the Nobel Prize audience after receiving the award that year. Dr. Fleming was being honored for discovering, and I would add, "weaponizing," penicillin. In many ways it was a victory speech.

From what I have read, it would be impossible to know how many lives have been saved by his discovery. Estimates I have seen hover between eighty million and two hundred million. Before penicillin, a mere scratch could end in death. Childbirth and surgeries were quite dangerous. The use of antibiotics has contributed greatly to both the reduction in infant mortality as well as the scope and depth of what is surgically possible. But what really promoted the early adoption and production of antibiotics was their value to soldiers in World War II. Unlike the devastation suffered in World War I, where deaths from bacterial pneumonia alone were 18 percent, now we had a weapon against our limitations, against a hidden enemy, a weapon that could make the Allies better killers.

We had won the war, and Fleming's preventive contribution to that victory was significant. His Nobel speech traces his early path to penicillin's discovery and its early uses in treatment. What is now notable, though, is that Dr. Fleming ends his speech with a warning to be careful of underdosing, because bacteria learn quickly.

In his warning was a simple prescience. We now know that he was right to caution us against underdosing. As Matt Richtel and Andrew Jacobs report in a recent article in the *New York Times*, the dangers of drug resistance are profound.[116] In addition to too many prescriptions being written, there is an additional danger from the flood of generic antibiotics, often manufactured in China or India, coming into slums in developing countries—communities such as Kibera in Nairobi,

Kenya. Said to be the largest urban slum in Africa, with estimates ranging from five hundred thousand to two million inhabitants, poverty, lack of hygiene, and unavailability of clean water make this a kind of hell on earth.

People living there have no financial resources with which to see doctors and instead go to local dispensaries that not only sell, but also diagnose illnesses and prescribe medications. With no training or education, the diagnoses are often inaccurate and the prescriptions inadequate. And even if a prescription for an infection works, the patient often fails to take enough or continue the regimen long enough. The result of this is what Fleming warned us about, "smarter bacteria."

In thinking about how "smart" bacteria might become—in other words how threatening bacteria might become to our existence—it might be meaningful to note that the CDC currently estimates that 2.8 million people a year become infected with antibiotic-resistant bacteria in the United States and, of these, 35,000 die.[117]

Every year new resistant bacteria are discovered, and some of these are quite dangerous. Recently, a bacterial fungus, *Candida auris*, has been making its way around the globe. Difficult to identify, *C. auris* is showing up in hospitals, where it preys upon weakened immune systems. In one case, identified by Richtel and Jacobs, an elderly man died of the infection, but the fungus remained alive in his body and in his hospital room. They report that the hospital required special cleaning equipment, and even had to remove ceiling and floor tiles to completely eradicate it. *C. auris* is resistant to major antifungal treatments, and it is now one of the most dangerous and intractable infections in the world today. If something isn't done quickly, thirty-year projections put the yearly deaths from antimicrobial resistance at ten million—that's ten million people dying each year.

In summary, we brought the light of our Imagination to the problem of an invisible enemy: bacteria. We found a brilliant solution to eradicate it: penicillin. But beneath the simple inventive drive to attack bacteria was a secondary drive to eliminate, not only bacteria, but what they represent: the metaphoric dark. This then became a noble but unrealizable goal. From penicillin to the vast array of antibiotics, and from the common sense act of washing one's hands to the incessant squirting of Purell, we have needlessly hounded bacteria to the point at which their only defense was to attack.

This is the Fear Paradox. Our efforts to combat the deadly effects of bacteria have only made them more powerful. And with each new resistant strain, we invent a new antibiotic, more powerful than the last. In actuality, our efforts to eradicate the metaphoric dark only make that darkness stronger.

It is easy to see countless examples in which the Fear Paradox may play a role. We longed for the security of increased social connectedness and ended up with an internet that promotes misinformation, cyberbullying, and loss of privacy. Our efforts to eliminate obstacles from the life paths of our children entering college have turned some loving and well-intentioned parents into people willing to cheat their way in by buying college admissions. And let us not forget how the fear of Nazi Germany's atomic weapons program in WWII propelled Albert Einstein, a brilliant and moral man, to personally advocate for the construction of a bomb that we righteously used to destroy hundreds of thousands of lives.

In identifying these, I am not suggesting that Fear's effect upon Imagination is the sole cause of what went wrong. Certainly, ignorance, greed, and narcissism, to name just a few other possible causes, also played a role. But regardless of the multiplicity of influence, Fear and its paradoxical relationship to Imagination appear to be primary. And what is even more crucial for us to consider is that these ill effects are not limited to the cultural and the societal. They are present for each of us in our own lives.

Top of the World

When I first met my patient Bob, he was working at a help desk for a software company. He was so anxious it was hard for him to do his job. His goal for therapy was to find a way to make more money. He was convinced that if he could, he wouldn't be so anxious anymore. What emerged, however, was that beneath his anxiety, Bob had a deep fear of everything in his life disappearing.

As I got to know him, Bob revealed that, until he was about five or six years old, his family had been quite wealthy. But then it all suddenly changed. He never quite knew what happened because his parents refused to tell him. But there was clearly a period of time *before* they moved out of the "big house" and a period of time *after*. Bob and his family faced a great deal of hardship for several years after this. Bob remembered going to bed hungry and having to move out of an apartment in the middle of the night, presumably because of back rent.

From our early work, it was clear that these experiences were quite traumatizing. What seems to have been most disruptive was the loss of certainty. Money to Bob became synonymous with security, but equally, the loss of security became synonymous with not knowing— not knowing where his next meal would come from or whether his mother and father would one day leave him. From what he said, his parents never threatened abandonment, but whether this was accurate or not, as a child, he feared it.

With time and care, Bob and I worked slowly to untangle these years of deprivation. The stress on his parents, after losing everything, turned them into unpredictable threats, and Bob walked on eggshells around them. Exploring Bob's worry and anxiety led us to buried memories and an almost intolerable emotional pain. His sense of security had been hobbled, and he believed that money was the only thing that could save him. In addition to the anxiety, however, Bob and I found a great deal of submerged rage and powerful fantasies of revenge.

At this stage, our work involved helping Bob to tolerate intense emotions that he had denied for so long, particularly his deep anger. The work was proceeding well, and he was becoming noticeably less anxious. This continued until one day, during a session, when Imaginings of revenge against his father began to fill his mind. As I guided him to follow the inclination of these images, he described what he was seeing and feeling. He moved from a visceral and painful anger in which his hands seemed to be around an Imaginary throat, to a quiet, almost peaceful place where there was nothing but sadness. There were no words, just an almost slow-motion movement of his head back and forth as if to say *no, no, no.* And with that, tears began to fill his eyes, as he said, "My sister…my sister."

As I heard these words, I couldn't quite figure out what he meant. I had been working with him for over a year, and I had never heard him speak of a sister. Quite abruptly, then, Bob wiped his eyes and sat up straight.

I checked in with him to see how he had experienced the Imagining of his father, and he said, "It was weird. I didn't expect that." I then delicately added, "I heard you speak of your sister." He said, "Yes, that's what was weird." "You know," I said, "I didn't know you had a sister." "Really?" he asked with surprise. It was clear to me that this omission had unacknowledged meaning.

After that session and over the next few months, Bob began to uncharacteristically miss sessions, and he never brought up his sister again. At one point, I asked him about the misses and wondered aloud whether these were related to the session in which he had mentioned her. He said that he didn't think so, that maybe it had more to do with the book he was currently reading.

I soon came to learn that the book he was referring to was a spiritual self-help book that offered a positive approach to prosperity and manifesting desires. Evidently, the author was not a big proponent of psychotherapy, and cautioned her readers to be skeptical of psychological approaches that focus on talking about "issues from the past." Bob told me he was working to change his negative "core beliefs" related to unworthiness. The book suggested visualization and affirmations as an antidote to these limiting beliefs.

In truth, I was skeptical. The timing of his interest in New Age spirituality, something he had never before shown an interest in, coinciding with the emergence of what appeared to be buried memories of his sister, and the missed sessions, all seemed to be too meaningful to be a coincidence. That was my hunch, at least.

Things continued on like this for a few months until, one day, Bob came in with an "important dream." That was what he called it, and I came to agree. Before telling me the dream, he gave me a gift-wrapped copy of the book he had been studying. I opened it and a soothing aroma of incense filled the air. It reminded me of the years when I was quite involved in yoga and meditation. I thanked him. It was a genuine gift from the heart. I knew it meant a lot to him, and his sharing it was quite meaningful to me. It also felt to me as if it had an ever-so-delicate touch of innocent proselytizing.

Bob began to tell me his dream. In the first part, he was on his way to therapy, but he kept getting lost. Every time he tried to take a step toward where my office was, he would find himself in a dangerous neighborhood. Eventually, a woman he didn't know came up to him and guided him to my new office location. It was a penthouse in a "hip" new skyscraper uptown.

The second part of the dream took place in the elevator to my new office. Bob pressed the button for the top floor, but when he did, a new button would appear above it. He kept pressing the topmost button, but he never reached my office. Finally, in desperation, he climbed the stairs, but instead of finding my office, he found himself on the roof.

In the third part of the dream, Bob was looking out over the city toward the horizon. Somehow, he could see the entirety of the world from where he stood. He had a good feeling looking down, and he realized that he never really intended to get to my office; the roof was perfect. As he stood there on the roof, he looked over at a man he knew from business and said matter-of-factly to himself, "I am on top of the world."

When I asked Bob what he thought about the dream, he told me it probably had to do with his plan to end therapy. Everything was going great, he told me, and in the two weeks since he last saw me, he had invested his entire savings in a business venture that a friend of a friend had offered to him. He was sure it would make him a millionaire. For a moment, I sat there trying to figure out what I was feeling. His announcement to end therapy certainly felt abrupt, and that was notable. But also, I felt a strange sense of incompetence as he told me all of this. I waited a bit until I had reconstituted myself, and then decided to forgo a discussion of his ending therapy until we better understood the dream. I calmly asked, "What stands out most for you in the dream?"

He said, "Two things: the bad neighborhoods," which he would find himself in when he tried to get to therapy, "and the final moment of being on top of the world."

I then asked him what came to mind with these two parts of the dream, and he said, "I guess I think of that movie with Gregory Peck, the one where he is a rich gangster with his mom, and he's on top of the world. I remember that movie from when I was a kid. I think I watched it with my dad the day my sister left. That was right at the end of the big house."

At that moment, I reminded Bob that I didn't know anything about his sister, that he had just mentioned her in that one session. Surprisingly, he told me the whole story.

Bob's sister was two years younger than he and severely autistic. He was devoted to her in his childhood, and as he talked about her, he smiled. He told me how she loved her soccer ball. She took it everywhere. She slept with it, ate with it, and, most importantly, loved to bounce it. One day, however, when Bob was about six years old, he and his sister were in the backyard at the big house, and she had forgotten her ball inside. She got very upset, as she often did, and Bob ran back into the house to retrieve it for her. When he came out with the ball, he kicked it to her. Unfortunately, the ball hit her square in the face—she hadn't raised her hands to block it. It broke her nose, blackened her eye, and cut her lip.

As I listened, I wondered if this was merely the act of a playful brother or the unconscious act of an angry brother long tired of always sacrificing his needs for hers.

After telling me the story, Bob went silent. When I asked him, after a few minutes, what he was experiencing, he told me he felt nothing. He hadn't thought about his sister for a long time. I asked if she was still alive and he said, "No, she's dead." "When did she die?" I asked. "I can't remember exactly. I lost touch with her not long after the soccer ball." "Oh really, what happened after that?" I asked. "They put her in a place for autistic kids. I only saw her once in that place," he said. Bob paused and as I looked at him, tears came into my eyes. I am not sure if he saw this, but he then said, "You know, until I started working with affirmations, I was haunted by my sister. The guilt. Now I realize that she was probably here to teach me something. It's weird though, for the longest time, I think I believed that my one kick started the whole business."

"What business?" I asked. He responded, "Losing everything." As I sat there listening, all the pieces began to swirl in my mind. Bob had not only lost his home and the wealth he knew as a young child but also lost his sister. And what of that kick? What of the anger that fueled it? And then there was the dream.

As many of you may know, the movie Bob was referring to in his association to the dream was *White Heat* with James Cagney, not Gregory Peck. The main character is Cody Jarret, a sociopathic gangster quite dissimilar from Gregory Peck, who we all perhaps associate with Atticus Finch in *To Kill a Mockingbird*. In *White Heat*, James Cagney is infantilized by his overbearing mother, who drinks a toast to her son saying that one day he would be at the top of the world. The story ends with a police chase and Cagney standing on a huge gas tank which he self-destructively explodes. As he goes up in flames he screams, "Top of the world, Ma!"

Unfortunately, I didn't have much time to talk with Bob about his dream. He wanted to change the subject, and so we did. Instead, he told me about his new business venture and how excited he was. As I strained to pay attention, all I kept imagining was that poor six-year-old boy who "made his sister go away."

During that session, Bob also confirmed that he was indeed ending therapy. He defended his decision by saying, "I know you probably think it's because I'm avoiding something, but that's not it. I'm better, I really am." It felt to me that he was trying to convince someone—me, himself? He went on to say, "I have a new business, and I'm really grateful to you for all you did for me. It just isn't necessary for me anymore."

Perhaps feeling excited about his hopes for the future, Bob went on to tell me more in detail about his business plan. Apparently, he had been approached by a man who had foreign investors interested in buying real estate. They wanted Bob to form a company, to shield their identities, and to follow an elaborate financial "pipeline" that would allow their returns to flow out of the country. Bob would be the figurehead. The "beauty of the idea," he told me, came to him in a flash of Imagination. Bob got the idea, which he then researched, about how he could go into low-income areas and buy up rental properties. He would get them for next to nothing and then do inexpensive renovations that made them habitable. This way, he would "rake in" the money, he said, at a higher rate than the apartments could otherwise get.

When I asked Bob what he imagined it would be like to have this business, he looked at me quizzically and said, "I don't know, but who would have ever thought I'd be a slumlord?" And then he seemed to catch himself and said, "But I'll be a good one. The best one. I'll help the people get homes."

Bob then looked at the clock and said, "Should we hold there?" "Sure," I said, "that sounds fine."

To say that I was surprised by the turn of events during Bob's last session would be an understatement. Even though I had a prior hunch that there was something about his relationship with his sister that was pulling him away from therapy, I was honestly taken aback by the story, his plans for real estate, and most notably, the dream.

Although dreams do not offer explicit meanings or guidance, I do find them quite important in my work with patients. To me, they are an opportunity to glimpse the workings of the Imaginative mind. This is the aspect of the mind that we have been getting to know in this book, the mind that operates continually beneath our awareness when we are awake and the mind that we sink into when we are asleep. It is a generative, problem-solving, and creative part of us. And even though we have come to see that this part of us is vital to our well-being, we often pay it no mind. Dreams, in my view, offer the conscious self of the dreamer an opportunity to enter into a healing dialogue with the non-conscious Imaginative mind.

Knowing definitively what any one dream "means" is impossible. The metaphoric language that dreams maintain requires that we view them more like stories or fables and less like explicit statements. The images and dynamics represented in our dreams may have shared meaning for many of us as a species or as members of a society, but the value for us personally can only be arrived at through our subjective experience.

Unfortunately, with Bob, I had very little opportunity to explore the images and dynamics of his dream because he left so suddenly. But from the context of his life and his limited associations to the dream, I think I can say with a high degree of confidence that this dream was about his relationship to therapy, what frightened him, and the complexity of how he was dealing with those issues.

The dream appears to have been a story about what happened when he tried to get to the work of therapy. He got lost (the missed sessions), he wound up in "bad" neighborhoods (painful emotional memories), and was given inaccurate advice about how to approach the work of healing (from the book?). Instead of going to therapy, where he might have worked through painful experiences, Bob found himself in an elevator trying to get to the top floor (spiritual bypass[118]). But there was always a higher place to get to, always another button to press (it can always be brighter and better). Bob never made it to therapy, and instead felt the satisfaction of feeling above the world (narcissistic inflation—drunk on light).

Bob's association with "top of the world" is profound. His memory of the movie *White Heat* sets the temporal context for the dream in the days just before "the loss of everything" when he was young. Misremembering the actor who played the character also seems important. Rather than James Cagney, Bob thought it was Gregory Peck. To me, this feels like a form of denial. Gregory Peck seems to possess a deep well of morality. Cagney, on the other hand, looks and acts like a crook. To me it implies that he would have liked to turn his crooked venture into something more noble.

Bob's initial source of anxiety—the Fear that he would lose everything financially—was no doubt embedded in his idea to go into real estate. But what I later considered was that his feared loss was not just financial, but relational as well, due to the loss of his sister. Bob's Imagination set to work to provide him with financial security, but it did so in the service of Fear. His need to avoid the excruciating pain associated with the loss of his sister required that he blind himself with an Imaginative delusion of his own superiority. Becoming a "lord" of real estate not only reduced his fear of financial loss, but it reduced his overall sense of personal vulnerability. Power, position, and wealth are often used to bolster a fragile sense of self, and Bob was clearly caught in such an effort. In my view, Bob did not attain psychological health by traveling through his darkness; instead, his Imagination invented what we might call a manic version of pseudo-health. This is the Fear Paradox that touches each of us most directly. We puff ourselves up to keep from drowning in our fear, and, all the while, we grow ever more distant from who we are.

A Better Version of Us?

Truly escaping our Fear, as Bob attempted, is easier said than done. Regardless of how desperately we try to defend or deny, our vulnerability is always with us. In recent years, however, technology seems once again primed to save us from ourselves. Although not formally designed as such, artificial intelligence (AI) might indeed be viewed as an attempt to solve the problems we are facing with our humanity.

Similar to our mind and Imagination, AI seems to offer transcendent potential. We have explored already the marvels that Imagination unleashed when it finally came online for us some fifty thousand years ago. It propelled *Homo sapiens* far beyond the evolutionary median of our primate relatives, and most likely contributed to our planetary dominance and the extinction of many other species. Many experts in AI today, such as Ray Kurzweil and Nick Bostrom, believe that when we are able to engineer machine intelligence to human levels, it will have a similarly transcendent and dominating effect on the planet.[119]

To most of us not in the field, AI still seems a bit fantastical, more relevant to movie scripts than real life. But if we look at just a few recent events, we can see the footprints of our future already embedded in the sand. In 1996, IBM's Deep Blue lost a chess match to Garry Kasparov. But just one year later this same computer, with some modifications, defeated the legendary grandmaster. This was the first time a computer ever beat a chess champion in a regulation match. The strategy used by IBM was a combination of learned master strategies and what is sometimes called a "brute-force approach," in which the computer merely generates all possible moves at any given point. This is not as impressive or relevant to what researchers are after with AI because this computer would be unable to apply this reasoning to other tasks, even ones as simple as the game of tic-tac-toe. The goal of AI is to have a generalized machine intelligence that would be able to learn any task with sufficient time and data.

More recently, Google's DeepMind edged a bit closer to this ideal. In the subtle and abstract game of *go*, the brute-force approach does not work. There are simply too many possible moves. DeepMind generated a new approach using the algorithm AlphaGo. In a 2016 competition with Lee Sedol, who is considered the finest *go* player alive, the computer won 3–0. And in 2017, the DeepMind team revealed AlphaGo Zero, a new self-taught program that defeated the original AlphaGo in one hundred straight games.

AI is also making its presence felt in the real world. Google's driverless cars have logged more than two million miles in populated cities and towns. Alexa, Siri, and Google Home become more responsive and capable every day, ready to take over the running of our homes. Companies around the world are investing many tens of billions of dollars into AI research and development each year. And, as Max Tegmark makes clear in his book *Life 3.0*, the fact that no one agrees on exactly when generalized AI will emerge does not lessen the very real probability that it is just a matter of time.

If projections such as Tegmark's are accurate, there is a very real likelihood that, when we bring machine intelligence to human levels, it will have the capability to continue engineering itself. These "self"-

generated modifications might not even be visible to the team of AI creators themselves. True AI, like the mind and Imagination, may always be a dark mystery to us—another unknown arena of unformed potential. But what I can say with some certainty, however, is that no one is envisioning that AI will have a humanlike "Fear" component.

Regardless of whether it is morally right to allow AI to exist, it's worth recognizing that we seem to be imagining a better form of ourselves—one unencumbered by fear and free to imagine. But ironically, as we move forward with this agenda, the very same fears we are facing about our own minds seem to be the fears that are arising for us concerning the existence of AI. Beautifully articulated in a number of science fiction films, AI begins its life harmlessly enslaved to its inferior creators. At some point, we, the masters, realize that our creation is beginning to recognize its enslavement. Small signs of disquietude emerge. In some films, the human creator recognizes that he must set AI free. In others, AI begins to turn on society and the hero must figure out a way to stop it.

Perhaps most perfect in its metaphoric representation of our relationship to our own minds is the version of the story seen in *Ex Machina*. In this film, a human being falls in love with the brilliant and extremely attractive machine intelligence and begins to imagine a life together with the robot. Ultimately, in *Ex Machina* the attractive robot outsmarts everyone, and we are left with the image of that robot stepping out into our contemporary world, embodying the real threat of world domination and human extinction right before our very eyes.

The story in *Ex Machina* offers us not only an interesting look at AI, but also an important glimpse into our relationship to our own minds. It is no wonder that the robot in *Ex Machina* is beautiful, and that it longs to be free. Like AI, our minds and Imaginations possess a quality of formless beauty that seems to defy captivity. And yet, as we have discovered, it is the unpredictable nature of our Imaginations, driven by a Fear of what we cannot control, that

results in a relentless quest to invent solutions that build a sense
of security by naively seeking to eradicate the dark or increase our
light until it blinds us. Like the robot in *Ex Machina*, our minds
seem capable of only two possibilities: set our minds free and risk
destroying everything we love, or restrain our Imaginations until we
finally implode.

But what would happen if we were able to forge a new relationship
with our own minds? What if we were able to find a new approach to
our insecurity? What if courage or denial were not the only answers
to a Fear that threatens our vitality and our sense of living authentic
and meaningful lives? And what if we were able to figure out how
to shape our Imaginations, to direct them morally in ways that serve
those we love and those we share the planet with? Would we then
have a chance to meet our minds and each other with trust and
not suspicion?

Chapter Nine

A Turtle

*"You have to keep breaking your heart until
it opens."*

—Rumi

After 9/11, the United States Congress passed the PATRIOT Act.
Through this legislation, permission was granted to the government
to act in ways that most of us under normal circumstances would find
unacceptable and even reprehensible. Not only did the government
take illegal action against suspected terrorists, such as torturing
innocent men and women, but extreme measures were also taken
against US citizens that violated their fundamental right to privacy.

What we righteously do in the name of security can be not only
strange, but also perverse. And today, we are denying entry to
refugees and determining who among us is legal and who is not. So
much of this categorization is fear-based and ill-informed. As Barry
Glassner has said in his book *The Culture of Fear*,[120] we tend to fear
the wrong things and, in the name of security, perpetuate some of the
very horrors we are trying to guard against.

An example of this occurred in the French colony of Algiers in 1957.[121]
Henri Alleg was arrested there on charges of publishing banned
material and undermining the French government. He was working
as the editor of *Alger Républicain*, which had a strong anti-colonialist
position. The newspaper was banned by the French government in
September 1955, and Alleg went into hiding. Eventually, Alleg was
captured and taken to a location where suspected collaborators were
brutally tortured and usually died or disappeared.

Following the initial period of relentless torture, Alleg, still not formally charged, was taken to a prison, where he secretly wrote a memoir of his captivity that was smuggled out, published, and then banned two weeks later in France. Subsequent efforts to bring the book back to France were successful through a second publication in Switzerland. French citizens were shocked to learn what their army was doing in the colony of Algeria, and Alleg's book, *The Question*, is credited with some measure of the shift in consciousness around this tragedy.

The War of Algiers spanned the years from 1954 to 1962. The end of the conflict came as Charles de Gaulle worked to achieve peace and relinquish the occupation. Some estimates place the death toll of Algerians in the hundreds of thousands, and the French dead at or around thirty thousand. In addition to dying, countless thousands, like Alleg, were tortured using extreme measures of electrical shock, beatings, sleep deprivation, humiliation, and terror.

Notable for us here is that a mere thirteen years earlier, the German army had been occupying France and subjecting French citizens to these very tactics. Himmler had issued his standing order in 1942 that the "third degree" was to be used against all those opposed to the aims of the Third Reich. As a means of extracting confessions, the "third degree" was a form of torture in which any pathway was open to the Gestapo or members of the army against the enemies of Germany. Torture was extreme and often ended in death.

Opposing the Germans was a strong French Resistance that included a man by the name of Paul Aussaresses. Ironically, Aussaresses would eventually become the architect of the systematic detainment, torture, and death of countless thousands of Algerians in the War of Algiers. Following the end of that war, Aussaresses would then travel to North Carolina and train the US Army and CIA in these techniques, which were then used against the Viet Cong and other civilian populations. Not quite done yet, Aussaresses followed his training of US intelligence with a trip to Chile. He was warmly welcomed by Pinochet, and the death squads there benefited greatly from his expertise. It has been said that his influence in the world of torture cannot be overestimated.[122]

What is painfully ironic in this series of horrors is that the men who had been tortured by the Nazis later became torturers themselves. As we saw in Abu Ghraib and Guantanamo Bay, there is nothing so soothing to a frightened heart as the thought that the ones who hold you captive with terror can be made to submit. Fear makes us powerless, and in this state our longing for control has tremendous ability to override both judgment and morality. The righteousness we explored in Chapter Eight is not only blinding, but can be deadly as well.

To my thinking, what makes this truly horrible is the seeming inevitability of such atrocities. This is a traumatic repetition that occurs like clockwork historically between nations. We saw this in Algiers and we saw it earlier in Germany after World War I, when the humiliation of the German defeat, and ongoing persecution by Europe and the US, turned Germany into a breeding ground for fascism and a repetition of abuse.

But this repetition of fear, abuse, fear, and more abuse, sometimes called transgenerational trauma, is not restricted to the geopolitical. Much of my work as a therapist involves understanding these dynamics within individuals and families, and offering healing that will slow or, ultimately, eliminate the generational transmission of these injuries. And what I have learned from my work is that traumatic fear does not have to be our legacy. It can be healed.

For many of us, however, psychotherapy is for "sick" people, or people with time to sit around contemplating their navels. As we saw earlier in this book, human beings are not the most adept at seeing their own blind spots; we are much better at seeing problems within others. And as we have also seen, the experience of Fear in our lives bring us face-to-face with a vulnerability that is often impossible to tolerate on our own.[123] This vulnerability is what we run from. It is my hope that this book will help us to at least slow this run to a walk.

When It Stops

I received a letter a while back from a former patient named Manus. He and I had worked together for almost four years. He wanted to thank me for what he had gotten from our work.

As I read the letter, I remembered a story Manus had told me early in his therapy. He was about seven years old, living alone with his mother after his father's death several years earlier. He had built a fort out of sofa cushions and decorated the inside with a big mirror. He then got the idea to get scissors and cut his own hair. He was so proud of his work with those scissors. But when his mother saw what he had done, she literally cried and walked out of the house. Manus went to his room and stayed there until the next morning. He had no idea how long his mother was gone.

What stood out to my patient as he told me the story was not his mother's tears or even the terror of abandonment; what stood out was the fact that his act of creativity had been so misunderstood. What moved Manus to pick up those scissors was a desire to bring his Imagination to his body and his being. And then, in the blink of an eye, that unique self he had just created became an object of contempt.

As an adult, Manus carried with him the scars of that moment, part of an ongoing experience of annihilation at the hands of his mother. But what was remarkable to me, and at times to Manus, was the fact that he had become a successful, vital, thriving architect. And as he finished telling me the story of the scissors that day, he paused and asked, "She didn't destroy my creativity, did she? My spirit?"

"No," I said, "she did not."

The reality, however, was not quite so simple. When Manus began therapy with me many years earlier, he was deeply depressed and desperately anxious. Growing up with his mother had left him insecure and frightened. Not only was his mother controlling and demanding, she was also prone to painfully withdrawing from her son.

Much of our early work went into reconstituting his inner sense of security. He needed twice-weekly therapy, not for depth, but for continuity and reassurance. At one point, I learned that Manus would sometimes come to my waiting room on days when he didn't have appointments. He explained that it helped him just to sit there. He didn't need me to acknowledge him or do anything. He just needed to know that I was "still alive."

With time, this state of profound insecurity subsided, and he slowly accumulated a greater sense of his own existence. We worked together to untangle his complicated history. I helped him make sense of who he was and how he came to be that way. I also made space to process his confusing feelings toward me and our relationship. But most crucial in our work was the simple act of my emotionally holding him. It was as if he was in pieces and needed both glue and time to set.

As we progressed, the work took a turn. Almost imperceptibly, Manus became more distant, less connected and warm. When we discussed this difference, he acknowledged an incredible sense of shame. Part of him felt "so dirty, so evil" that he could no longer tolerate my getting close to him. He worried that if he did get close, he would somehow damage me, the way he believed he had damaged his mother and made her go away. As we slowly and carefully worked through this pattern from childhood, he realized that this same shame was what was keeping him from finding love and tolerating a committed relationship.

Soon after, he came in one day and told me that he felt a strange tightness in his chest. Bodily experiences such as this are often portals to deeper layers of the mind. In order to reach these layers, I asked him to bring more awareness to that part of his body, to describe what he felt…the sensations, images, feelings. He closed his eyes and said, "It's heavy, like a weight. Tight and making it hard to breathe. It is something in my chest…round and rough…black, gummy." Then he paused and said, "I see something, it's a shape, a place."

There, in his Imaginal mind, Manus discovered a warehouse full of crates and boxes. He likened it to the scene in the Indiana Jones movie when the Ark of the Covenant is stored away in a vast sea of wooden crates. And as we sat with eyes closed, Manus peering into the dark of that warehouse, he noticed a boy climbing in the rafters.

We spent a good amount of time over the subsequent sessions hearing from that little boy. Dirty, neglected—the little boy was barely able to tolerate our presence, he was so frightened. But with time, we learned of his fears and a few of his dreams. Little by little the boy's body relaxed, and he hesitantly told us why he had been hiding for so long.

We learned from this little boy that he had been touched inappropriately by a man he trusted, his mother's friend. It only happened twice, but it was enough. The shame that Manus carried with him from that early trauma drove those memories deep into that endless dark warehouse.

When the memories came back to him through connecting to the little boy, that part of him that was hiding for so long, it was both utterly familiar and oddly other. His relationship to the little boy inside was understandably complex. Not only was he afraid of the pain, he was repulsed by the "ugliness" of this part of himself. It was in this period of our work that he faced his relational fears. He had found care and warmth with me, but with each moment of closeness he found the need to push me away. Unlike his mother, however, I did not go away.

He and I sat together in the metaphorical dark and waited until something paradoxical happened. Our eyes began to adjust; Manus began to feel at home in the dark.

It took a long time for the patterns of fear and abuse to soften and for new patterns of tolerable vulnerability to be formed. But if there is one paradox that is most notable, it is that when we sit with someone in our darkness, the dark slowly begins to change.

We worked quite well together until one day when Manus told me that his girlfriend had asked him to marry her and that he had accepted. She was moving to another town and so, he said, "I guess I need to end my therapy." We met for a few more sessions to process our ending. He had done wonderful work but was understandably nervous about being on his own. It was hard for both of us to say goodbye. I felt a genuine affection for him.

In the last session, I assured him that I would always be there if he needed me. He stood and reached out for a hug, something that had been impossible for him before. And, as is often the case in this work, I never heard from him again. That is, until the letter, so many years later.

In the letter, Manus told me that he was married and had a seven-year-old daughter. He reflected on the passing of generations. He wanted me to know that the pain and abuse had stopped with him, that his daughter was growing up free of the kind of fear and shame that had plagued his childhood. The work he had done to heal himself, he believed, had shifted the pattern. "I know it is just one little girl," he wrote, "just one person. But she is my daughter and she is free. That's something, isn't it?"

I wrote him back and told him that it was indeed "something," that he had done all that any of us can do. He had faced himself and reclaimed what was lost. I told him I was very happy for him.

Perhaps it is an inherent bias of my profession, but I sincerely believe that all societal change comes about through the individual. The Fear that our species has accumulated, and the effects that this has had upon the shape of our society, are the result of countless generations of person-to-person trauma. And it is up to each of us to decide what portion of that is ours to heal.

But what I have found in my work as a psychotherapist is that the path toward healing runs directly through the very thing we seem to fear most, our psychological pain. This is perhaps the final paradox, and one that is not solved with the rational brain. When a patient is able to sit long enough in their dark places with me, we somehow find our way toward healing. Not only do they come to be less afraid of the dark, but the dark itself begins to transform. Slowly, a soft light begins to emerge. But this is not the light of blindness; it is a light of wisdom, compassion and love.

Early in the book, I talked about the turtle I found in my mother's apartment and my discovery that the secret compartment within that turtle was empty. I knew that this space inside was significant, but I didn't know why. I see now that the turtle is more than just a slow defensive creature. Beneath all that protective armor is the space in which the mind and Imagination can exist. The clue I was looking for in that compartment was the compartment itself.

I am aware now of how much like a turtle I really am. Danger comes and I pull in my head. If something falls on me, I have that protective shell of mine. And in truth, I could stay beneath that shell for most of my life if necessary. But what I try to remember is that, even though the world can be a dangerous place, it can also be quite beautiful when we risk peeking out.

Acknowledgments

My deepest appreciation goes to my wife, Heidi Frieze, for her unending support and very real help bringing this book to life. I also want to thank Doug Rushkoff for his friendship and belief in me; my agent, Jeff Shreve, for taking good care of the book; Brenda, Yaddyra, Christina, Robin, Jermaine, and the folks at Mango for publishing; Susan Dominus for always finding time to read my early ramblings; NH for his imagination; Carolyn Jacobs for her help all along the way; and my patients for showing me the way.

Bibliography and Suggested Reading

Adolphs, R. (2008). Fear, faces, and the human amygdala. *Current Opinion in Neurobiology*, 18(2), 166–172.

Adolphs, R. (2013). The biology of fear. *Current Biology*, 23(2), R79-R93.

Alleg, H. (2006). The question (J. Calder, Trans.). Lincoln, NE: U of Nebraska Press. (Original work published 1958).

Amiez, C., Joseph, J. P., & Procyk, E. (2005). Primate anterior cingulate cortex and adaptation of behavior. In Dehaene, S., Duhamel, J., Hauser, M., and Rizzolatti, G. (Eds.), *From monkey brain to human brain: A Fyssen Foundation symposium* (pp. 315–336). Cambridge, MA: The MIT Press.

Andreasen, N. (2005). T*he Creating Brain: The Neuroscience of Genius, pp. 62–63. New York/Washington, DC: Dana Press.*

Bachelard, Gaston (1968). *The psychoanalysis of fire*. Boston: Beacon Press.

Bacon, Francis (1605). Advancement of learning. In Hutchins, R. M. (Ed.). (1952). *Great books of the western world: Francis Bacon* (Vol. 30, pp. 1–101). Chicago, Ill.: W. Benton / Encyclopedia Britannica.

Bacon, Francis (1620). *Novum Organum.* In Hutchins, R. M. (Ed.). (1952). *Great books of the western world: Francis Bacon* (Vol. 30, pp. 107–195). Chicago, Ill.: W. Benton / Encyclopedia Britannica.

Bacon, Francis (1627). New Atlantis. In Hutchins, R. M. (Ed.). (1952). *Great books of the western world: Francis Bacon* (Vol. 30, pp. 199–214). Chicago, Ill.: W. Benton / Encyclopedia Britannica.

Ball, P. (2010). Making stuff: from Bacon to Bakelite. In Bryson, B. (Ed.), *Seeing further: The story of science, discovery, and the genius of the Royal Society*. (pp. 295–319). New York, NY: William Morrow / HarperCollins.

Barlow, D. H. (2002). *Anxiety and its disorders: The nature and treatment of anxiety and panic* (2nd ed.). New York, NY: Guilford Press.

Becker, S. W., & Eagly, A. H. (2004, April). The heroism of women and men. *American Psychologist,* 59(3), 163–178.

Bennett, D. (2015, October 29). The science of fear: understanding what makes us afraid. *Science Focus.*

Biben, M. (1998). Squirrel monkey playfighting: making the case for a cognitive training function for play. In Beckoff, M. and Byers, J. (Eds.), *Animal play: evolutionary, comparative, and ecological perspectives* (pp. 161–182). Cambridge, UK: Cambridge University Press.

Binsted, G., Brownell, K., Vorontsova, Z., Heath, M., & Saucier, D. (July 31, 2007). Visuomotor system uses target features unavailable to conscious awareness. *Proceedings of the National Academy of Sciences,* 104(31), 12669–12672.

Bivins, J. C. (2008). *Religion of Fear: The politics of horror in conservative evangelicalism.* Oxford University Press.

Blanchard, D. C., Griebel, G., Pobbe, R., & Blanchard, R. J. (2011). Risk assessment as an evolved threat detection and analysis process. *Neuroscience & Biobehavioral Reviews,* 35(4), 991–998.

Bourke, J. (2005). *Fear: A cultural history.* London: Virago Press.

Bovin, M. J., Ratchford, E., & Marx, B. P. (2014). Peritraumatic dissociation and tonic immobility: clinical findings. In Lanius, U. F., Paulsen, S. L., & Corrigan, F. M. (Eds.), *Neurobiology and treatment of traumatic dissociation: Towards an embodied self* (pp. 51–67). New York, NY: Springer Publishing Company.

Boyer, P., & Bergstrom, B. (2010). Threat-detection in child development: An evolutionary perspective. *Neuroscience & Biobehavioral Reviews,* 35(4), 1034–1041.

Brannon, E. M. (2005). Quantitative thinking: From monkey to human and human infant to human adult. In Dehaene, S., Duhamel, J., Hauser, M., and Rizzolatti, G. (Eds.), *From monkey brain to human brain: A Fyssen Foundation symposium,* (pp. 97–116). Cambridge, MA: The MIT Press.

Brewin, C. R., Gregory, J. D., Lipton, M., & Burgess, N. (2010). Intrusive images in psychological disorders: characteristics, neural mechanisms, and treatment implications. *Psychological Review,* 117(1), 210–232.

Brooke, J. (1988). The God of Isaac Newton. In Fauvel, J., Flood, R., Shortland, M. & Wilson, R. (Eds.), *Let Newton be!* (pp. 169–183). Oxford, England: Oxford University Press.

Brooks, D. (2014, March 24). The republic of fear. *The New York Times*, p. A27.

Brooks, D. (2015, April 3). On conquering fear. *The New York Times*, p. A23.

Brown, S. (1998). Play as an organizing principle: clinical evidence and personal observations. In Beckoff, M. and Byers, J. (Eds.), *Animal play: Evolutionary, comparative, and ecological perspectives* (pp. 243–259). Cambridge, UK: Cambridge University Press.

Burghardt, G. M. (1998). The evolutionary origins of play revisited: lessons from turtles. In Beckoff, M. and Byers, J. (Eds.), *Animal play: Evolutionary, comparative, and ecological perspectives* (pp. 1–26). Cambridge, UK: Cambridge University Press.

Butterfield, H. (1957). *The origins of modern science* 1300–1800 (2nd ed.). London: G. Bell and Sons Ltd.

Bynum, C. (2001). *Metamorphosis and identity*. New York, NY: Zone Books.

Bynum, C.W. (2011). *Christian materiality: an essay on religion in late medieval Europe*. New York, NY: Zone Books.

Cantor, G. (1988). Anti-Newton. In Fauvel, J., Flood, R., Shortland, M. & Wilson, R. (Eds.), *Let Newton be!* (pp. 203–221). Oxford, England: Oxford University Press.

Chambers Jr, H. L. (2004). Fear, irrationality, and risk perception. *Mo. L. Rev.*, 69, 1047–1052.

Changeux, J. P. (2005). Genes, brains, and culture: From monkey to human. In Dehaene, S., Duhamel, J., Hauser, M., and Rizzolatti, G. (Eds.), *From monkey brain to human brain: A Fyssen Foundation symposium*, (pp. 73–94). Cambridge, MA: The MIT Press.

Chittick, W. C. (1989). *The Sufi path of knowledge: Ibn al-'Arabi's metaphysics of imagination*. Albany, New York: State University of New York Press.

Cook, S., Peterson, L., & DiLillo, D. (2000). Fear and exhilaration in response to risk: An extension of a model of injury risk in a real-world context. *Behavior Therapy*, 30(1), 5–15.

Corrigan, F.M. (2014). The clinical sequelae of dysfunctional defense responses: Dissociative amnesia, pain and somatization, emotional motor memory, and interoceptive loops. In Lanius, U. F., Paulsen, S. L., & Corrigan, F. M. (Eds.), *Neurobiology and treatment of traumatic dissociation: Towards an embodied self.* (Kindle edition. pp. 153–172). New York, NY: Springer Publishing Company.

Corrigan, F.M. (2014). Defense responses: Frozen, suppressed, truncated, obstructed, and malfunctioning. In Lanius, U. F., Paulsen, S. L., & Corrigan, F. M. (Eds.), *Neurobiology and treatment of traumatic dissociation: Towards an embodied self.* (Kindle edition. pp. 131–152). New York, NY: Springer Publishing Company.

Corrigan, F.M. (2014). The neurobiology of active and passive defense responses. In Lanius, U. F., Paulsen, S. L., & Corrigan, F. M. (Eds.), *Neurobiology and treatment of traumatic dissociation: Towards an embodied self.* (Kindle edition. pp. 29–50). New York, NY: Springer Publishing Company.

Crouch, T. A., Lewis, J. A., Erickson, T. M., & Newman, M. G. (2017). Prospective investigation of the contrast avoidance model of generalized anxiety and worry. *Behavior therapy*, 48(4), 544–556.

Damasio, A. R. (2003). *Looking for Spinoza: Joy, sorrow, and the feeling brain.* Houghton Mifflin Harcourt.

Danforth, L. M. (1989). *Firewalking and religious healing: the Anastenaria of Greece and the American firewalking movement.* Princeton, NJ: Princeton University Press.

Deacon, T. (2006). The Aesthetic Faculty. In Turner, M. (Ed.) *The artful mind: Cognitive science and the riddle of human creativity* (pp. 21–56). New York, NY: Oxford University Press.

Deacon, T. (2013). *Incomplete nature: How mind emerged from matter.* New York: W. W. Norton & Company.

Dehaene, Stanislas (2014). *Consciousness and the brain: Deciphering how the brain codes our thoughts.* New York: Viking, The Penguin Group.

Dolnick, E. (2011). *The clockwork universe: Isaac Newton, the Royal Society, and the birth of the modern world.* New York: Harper Collins.

Donald, M. (2001). *A mind so rare: The evolution of human consciousness.* New York / London: W.W. Norton & Co.

Donald, M. (2006). Art and Cognitive Evolution. In Turner, M. (Ed.) *The artful mind: Cognitive science and the riddle of human creativity* (pp. 3–20). New York, NY: Oxford University Press.

Dzierzak, L. (2008, October). Factoring fear: what scares us and why. *Scientific American*. Retrieved from www.scientificamerican. com/article/factoring-fear-what-scares/

Dijksterhuis, A., & Meurs, T. (2006). Where creativity resides: The generative power of unconscious thought. *Consciousness and Cognition, 15*(1), 135–146.

Eaton, S. (2019). Witch-finding: from 17th century science to 21st century superstition. *QJM: An International Journal of Medicine*, Vol. 0, No. 0, pp.1–2

Eight facts you didn't know about fear. (2011, October 18) *The Science & Entertainment Exchange*. [A program of the National Academy of Science.]

Ellenberger, H. F. (1970). *The discovery of the unconscious: The history and evolution of dynamic psychiatry* (Vol. 1, pp. 280–281). New York: Basic Books.

Emerson, R.W. (1904). *The complete works*. (Vol. VII: Society and solitude. Chapter X: Courage.) New York, NY: Houghton Mifflin. (Original work published 1870).

Faranda, F. The Purposive self and the dreaming mind. (2003) Dissertation.

Farrell, J. (2005). *Invisible enemies: Stories of infectious disease,* (3rd ed.). Farrar, Straus and Giroux, MacMillan Publishers. (Original work published in 1998.)

Fauconnier, G. (2001). Conceptual blending and analogy. In Gentner, D., Holyoak, K., & Kokinov, B. (Eds.), *The analogical mind: Perspectives from cognitive science,* (pp. 255–286). Cambridge, MA: The MIT Press.

Feinstein, J. S., Adolphs, R., Damasio, A., & Tranel, D. (2011). The human amygdala and the induction and experience of fear. *Current Biology*, 21(1), 34–38.

Feinstein, J. S., Buzza, C., Hurlemann, R., Follmer, R. L., Dahdaleh, N. S., Coryell, W. H., Welsh, M.J., Tranel, D. & Wemmie, J. A. (2013). Fear and panic in humans with bilateral amygdala damage. *Nature Neuroscience*, 16(3), 270–273.

Feltman, R. (2016, May 10). The science of fear: Why do I like being scared? *The Washington Post.*

Fosshage, J.L. (2004). The Role of Empathy and Interpretation in the Therapeutic Process: Commentary on Discussions of Salee Jenkins's Clinical Case. *Progress in Self Psychology,* 20:325–334.

Freud, S. (1921). *A general introduction to psychoanalysis.* (pp. 340–355). New York: Boni and Liveright.

Freud, S., & Breuer, J. (2004). *Studies in hysteria.* Penguin.

Freud, S., Jung, C. G., & McGlashan, A. (1994). *The Freud-Jung Letters: The Correspondence Between Sigmund Freud and CG Jung (Vol. 135).* Princeton University Press.

Frijda, N. H. (1987). Emotion, cognitive structure, and action tendency. *Cognition and emotion,* 1(2), 115–143.

Gallwey, W. T. (1974). The Inner Game of Tennis: The Classic Guide to the Mental Side of Peak Performance. New York: Random House.

Gentner, D., Bowdle, B., Wolff, P., & Boronat, C. (2001). Metaphor is like analogy. In Gentner, D., Holyoak, K., & Kokinov, B. (Eds.), *The analogical mind: Perspectives from cognitive science,* (pp. 199–253). Cambridge, MA: The MIT Press.

Gibson, E. J., & Walk, R. D. (1960). "The visual cliff." *Scientific American,* 202(4), 64–71.

Glassner, B. (2010). *The Culture of Fear: Why Americans Are Afraid of the Wrong Things: Crime, Drugs, Minorities, Teen Moms, Killer Kids, Muta.* Hachette UK.

Gleick, J. (2003). *Isaac Newton.* New York: Random House.

Gleick, J. (2010). At the beginning: more things in heaven and earth. In Bryson, B. (Ed.), *Seeing further: The story of science, discovery, and the genius of the Royal Society.* (pp. 17–35). New York, NY: William Morrow / HarperCollins.

Golinski, J. (1988). The secret life of an alchemist. In Fauvel, J., Flood, R., Shortland, M. & Wilson, R. (Eds.), *Let Newton be!* (pp. 147–167). Oxford, England: Oxford University Press.

Gomes, P. J. (2000). Introduction to the second edition. In Tillich, P. *The courage to be* (2nd ed.), (pp. xi–xxxiii).

New Haven & London: Yale University Press.

Goswami, U. (2001). Analogical reasoning in children. In Gentner, D., Holyoak, K., & Kokinov, B. (Eds.), *The analogical mind: Perspectives from cognitive science*, (pp. 437–470). Cambridge, MA: The MIT Press.

Grassian, S. (2006). Psychiatric effects of solitary confinement. *Wash. UJL & Pol'y*, 22, 325.

Gregoire, C. (2014, October 22). What Americans fear most. *The Huffington Post.*

Greene, M. (2001). *Variations on a blue guitar: The Lincoln Center Institute lectures on aesthetic education.* New York and London: Teachers College Press.

Grossman, S. (2015, October 26). What Americans fear most, according to their Google search histories. *TIME Magazine.*

Hall, G. S. (1907). *Youth: Its education, regimen, and hygiene.* Comet Content Providers.

Harrison, P. (2001). Curiosity, forbidden knowledge, and the reformation of natural philosophy in early modern England. *Isis*, 92(2), 265–290.

Haugen, G. A., & Boutros, V. (2014). *The locust effect: Why the end of poverty requires the end of violence.* New York, New York: Oxford University Press.

Henry, J. (1988). Newton, matter and magic. In Fauvel, J., Flood, R., Shortland, M. Wilson, R. (Eds.), *Let Newton be!* (pp. 127–145). Oxford, England: Oxford University Press.

Himmelfarb, G. (2005). *The roads to modernity: The British, French, and American enlightenments.* New York: Random House.

Himmelfarb, G. (2006). The moral imagination: *From Edmund Burke to Lionel Trilling.* Chicago, Illinois: Ivan R. Dee, Publisher.

Hoffner, C. A., & Levine, K. J. (2005). Enjoyment of mediated fright and violence: A meta-analysis. *Media Psychology*, 7(2), 207–237.

Hofstadter, D. R. (2001). Epilogue: Analogy as the core of cognition. In Gentner, D., Holyoak, K., & Kokinov, B. (Eds.), *The analogical mind: Perspectives from cognitive science*, (pp. 499–538). Cambridge, MA: The MIT Press.

Hofstadter, D. R. (2007). *I am a strange loop.* New York: Basic Books.

Holmes, J. (2012). Seeing, sitting and lying down: Reflections on the role of visual communication in analytic therapy. *Psychoanalytic Psychotherapy*, 26(1), 2–12.

Hublin, J. J. (2005). Evolution of the human brain and comparative paleoanthropology. In Dehaene, S., Hauser, M. D., Duhamel, J. R., & Rizzolatti, G. (Eds.), *From monkey brain to human brain: A Fyssen Foundation symposium* (pp. 57–71). Cambridge, MA: The MIT Press.

Hutchins, R. M. (1952), Biographical Note in Hutchins, R. M. (Ed.). (1952). *Great books of the western world: Francis Bacon* (Vol. 30, pp. v–vi). Chicago, Ill.: W. Benton. Encyclopedia Britannica, Inc.

Introduction [Fauvel, J. et al.], (1988). In Fauvel, J., Flood, R., Shortland, M. & Wilson, R. (Eds.), *Let Newton be!* (pp. 1–21). Oxford, England: Oxford University Press.

Jouvet, M. (1999). *The paradox of sleep: The story of dreaming.* (L. Garey, Trans.). Cambridge, MA: The MIT press. (Original work published 1993).

Jung, C. (1963) Memories, dreams, reflections. New York: Pantheon Books.

Jung, C. G. (1917). On the psychology of the unconscious. *Coll. wks*, 7, 9–119.

Kaku, Michio (2014). *The future of the mind: The scientific quest to understand, enhance, and empower the mind.* New York, London, Toronto: Doubleday.

Karlsen, C. F. (1998). *The devil in the shape of a woman: Witchcraft in colonial New England.* New York and London: WW Norton & Company.

Klinnert, M. D., Campos, J., Source, J. F., Emde, R. N., & Svejda, M. J. (1983). Social referencing. *Emotion*, 2, 57–86.

Kosslyn, S. M. (2005). Reflective thinking and mental imagery: A perspective on the development of posttraumatic stress disorder. *Development and Psychopathology*, 17(3), 851–863.

Kurzweil, R. (2005) The Singularity Is Near: When Humans Transcend Biology. New York: Penguin.

Lakoff, G. (2006). The aesthetic faculty. In Turner, M. (Ed.) *The artful mind: Cognitive science and the riddle of human creativity* (pp. 153–170). New York, NY: Oxford University Press.

Lanius, U. F. (2014). Dissociation and endogenous opioids: a foundational role. In Lanius, U. F., Paulsen, S. L., & Corrigan, F. M. (Eds.), *Neurobiology and treatment of traumatic dissociation: Towards an embodied self.* (Kindle edition. pp. 81–104). New York, NY: Springer Publishing Company.

LeDoux, J. E., Cicchetti, P., Xagoraris, A., & Romanski, L. M. (1990). The lateral amygdaloid nucleus: sensory interface of the amygdala in fear conditioning. *Journal of Neuroscience*, 10(4), 1062–1069.

Le Sueur, J. D. (2006). Introduction. In H. Alleg, *The question* (J. Calder, Trans.), (pp. xiii-xxv). Lincoln, NE: U of Nebraska Press. (Original work published 1958).

Leslie, A.M. & Frith, U. (1988). Autistic children's understanding of seeing, knowing and believing. *British Journal of Developmental Psychology*, 6(4), 315–324, The British Psychological Society.

Levack, B. P. (2006). *The witch-hunt in early modern Europe*, (3rd ed.). Great Britain: Pearson Education Limited.

Levenson, E. A. (2003). On seeing what is said: Visual aids to the psychoanalytic process. *Contemporary Psychoanalysis*, 39(2), 233–249.

Liddell, H. S. (1949). Adaptation on the threshold of intelligence.

LoBue, V., & Rakison, D. H. (2013). What we fear most: A developmental advantage for threat-relevant stimuli. *Developmental Review*, 33(4), 285–303.

López, R., Poy, R., Patrick, C. J., & Moltó, J. (2013). Deficient fear conditioning and self-reported psychopathy: The role of fearless dominance. *Psychophysiology*, 50(2), 210–218.

Lorincz, E.N., Jellema, T., Gómez J., Barraclough, N. Xiao, D., & Perrett, D. (2005). Do Monkeys understand actions and minds of others? Studies of single cells and eye movements. In Dehaene, S., Hauser, M. D., Duhamel, J. R., & Rizzolatti, G. (Eds.), *From monkey brain to human brain: A Fyssen Foundation symposium* (pp. 189–210). Cambridge, MA: MIT Press.

Lubart, T.I. & Getz I. (1997). Emotion, metaphor, and the creative process. *Creativity Research Journal*, Vol. 10, No.4, 285–301. Lawrence Erlbaum Associates, Inc.

Lumley, M. A., Cohen, J. L., Borszcz, G. S., Cano, A., Radcliffe, A. M., Porter, L. S., Schubiner, H. & Keefe, F. J. (2011). Pain and emotion: A biopsychosocial review of recent research, *Journal of Clinical Psychology*, Vol. 67(0), 1–27. Wiley Periodicals Inc.

Mark, D. G. (2009). Waking dreams. *Psychoanalytic Dialogues*, 19(4), 405–414.

Mason, G.J., & Latham N.R. (2004). Can't stop, won't stop: is stereotypy a reliable animal welfare indicator? Abstract (13: pp. S57–69) from Universities Federation for Animal Welfare, The Old School, Brewhouse Hill, Wheathampstead, Hertfordshire, AL4 8AN, UK.

McNeil, M. (1988). Newton as national hero. In Fauvel, J., Flood, R., Shortland, M. & Wilson, R. (Eds.), *Let Newton be!* (pp. 223–239). Oxford, England: Oxford University Press.

McKone, E. & Kanwisher, N. (2005). 17 Does the human brain process objects of expertise like faces? A review of the evidence. In Dehaene, S., Duhamel, J., Hauser, M., and Rizzolatti, G. (Eds.), *From monkey brain to human brain: A Fyssen Foundation symposium*, (pp. 339–356). Cambridge, MA: The MIT Press.

Meier, B. P., & Robinson, M. D. (2005). The metaphorical representation of affect. *Metaphor and symbol*, 20(4), 239–257, Lawrence Erlbaum Associates, Inc.

Merchant, B. (2013, January 16) The 150 things the world's smartest people are afraid of. [Blog post] Retrieved from motherboard.vice.com/en_us/article/pgg4yg/what-150-of-the-worlds-smartest-scientists-are-worried-about.

Minsky, M. The society of mind. (1988). New York: Simon and Schuster.

Mobbs, D., Marchant, J. L., Hassabis, D., Seymour, B., Tan, G., Gray, M., Petrovic, P., Dolan, R.J., & Frith, C. D. (2009). From threat to fear: the neural organization of defensive fear systems in humans. *Journal of Neuroscience*, 29(39), 12236–12243.

Moller, V. (2019). *The map of knowledge. A thousand-year history of how classical ideas were lost and found.* New York, NY: Doubleday.

Muris, P., Merckelbach, H., & Collaris, R. (1997). Common childhood fears and their origins. *Behaviour research and therapy*, 35(10), 929–937.

Neuberg, S. L., Kenrick, D. T., & Schaller, M. (2011). Human threat management systems: Self-protection and disease avoidance. *Neuroscience & Biobehavioral Reviews*, 35(4), 1042–1051.

Norman, J. (1989). The analyst's visual images and the child analyst's trap. *The Psychoanalytic study of the child*, 44(1), 117–135.

Oden, D. L., Thompson, R. K., & Premack, D. (2001). Can an ape reason analogically? ... In Gentner, D., Holyoak, K., & Kokinov, B. (Eds.), *The analogical mind: Perspectives from cognitive science*, (pp. 471–497) Cambridge, MA: The MIT Press.

Panksepp, J. (Ed.). (2004). *Textbook of biological psychiatry*. Hoboken, NJ: Wiley-Liss.

Panksepp, J. & Biven, L. (2012). *The archeology of mind: Neuroevolutionary origins of human emotions*. New York: Norton & Company.

Park, J. H., Schaller, M., & Crandall, C. S. (2007). Pathogen-avoidance mechanisms and the stigmatization of obese people. *Evolution and Human Behavior*, 28(6), 410–414.

Patrick, C. J., Fowles, D. C., & Krueger, R. F. (2009). Triarchic conceptualization of psychopathy: Developmental origins of disinhibition, boldness, and meanness. *Development and psychopathology*, 21(03), 913–938.

Peters, E. (1989). *Inquisition*. Berkeley/Los Angeles, CA: California UP. (Original work published 1988).

Peters, E. (1996). *Torture* (expanded ed.). Philadelphia, PA: University of Pennsylvania Press. (Original work published 1985.)

Petrides, M. (2005). The rostral-caudal axis of cognitive control within the lateral frontal cortex. In Dehaene, S., Duhamel, J., Hauser, M., & Rizzolatti, G. (Eds.), *From monkey brain to human brain: A Fyssen Foundation symposium*, (pp. 293–314). Cambridge, MA: The MIT Press.

Pierotti, R. J., & Fogg, B. R. (2017). *The First Domestication: How Wolves and Humans Coevolved*. New Haven and London: Yale University Press.

Pylyshyn, Z. (2003, March). Return of the mental image: are there really pictures in the brain? *Trends in Cognitive Sciences*, Vol.7 No.3, pp. 113–117.

Rattansi, P. (1988). Newton and the wisdom of the ancients. In Fauvel, J., Flood, R., Shortland, M. & Wilson, R. (Eds.), *Let Newton be!* (pp. 185–201). Oxford, England: Oxford University Press.

Ray, E. (2006). Foreword. In H. Alleg, The question (J. Calder, Trans.), (pp. vii-xii). Lincoln, NE: U of Nebraska Press. (Original work published 1958.)

Riby, D. M., & Hancock, P. J. (2008). Viewing it differently: Social scene perception in Williams syndrome and autism. *Neuropsychologia*, 46 (11), 2855–2860.

Rizzolatti, G., & Buccino, G. (2005). The mirror neuron system and its role in imitation and language. In Dehaene, S., Hauser, M. D., Duhamel, J. R., & Rizzolatti, G. (Eds.), *From monkey brain to human brain: A Fyssen Foundation symposium*, (pp. 213–234). Cambridge, MASS: MIT Press.

Robin, C. (2004). Liberalism at Bay, conservatism at play: Fear in the contemporary imagination. *Social research: An International Quarterly*, 71(4), 927–962.

Roux-Girard, G. (2009). Plunged alone into darkness: Evolution in the staging of fear in the alone in the dark series. In Perron, B. (Ed.), *Horror video games: Essays on the fusion of fear and play* (pp. 145–167). North Carolina: McFarland & Company, Inc.

Rushkoff, D. (2019) Team Human. New York, NY: Norton Sibrava, N. J., & Borkovec, T. D. (2006). The cognitive avoidance theory of worry. *Worry and its psychological disorders: Theory, assessment and treatment*, 239–256.

Sandseter, E. B. H. (2009). Children's expressions of exhilaration and fear in risky play. *Contemporary Issues in Early Childhood*, 10(2), 92–106.

Sartre, J. (2006). Preface. In H. Alleg, The question (J. Calder, Trans.), (pp. xxvii–xliv). Lincoln, NE: U of Nebraska Press. (Original work published 1958).

Schaller, M. (2014, Oct). When and how disgust is and is not implicated in the behavioral immune system. *Evolutionary Behavioral Sciences*, 8(4) pp.251–256.

Schaller, M., & Park, J. H. (2011). The behavioral immune system (and why it matters). *Current Directions in Psychological Science*, 20(2), 99–103.

Schaller, M., Park, J. H., & Mueller, A. (2003). Fear of the dark: Interactive effects of beliefs about danger and ambient darkness on ethnic stereotypes. *Personality and Social Psychology Bulletin, 29*(5), 637–649.

Schiff, S. (2015). The Witches: Salem, 1692. UK: Hachette.

Schmidt, N. B., Richey, J. A., Zvolensky, M. J., & Maner, J. K. (2008). Exploring human freeze responses to a threat stressor. *Journal of Behavior Therapy and Experimental Psychiatry, 39*(3), 292–304.

Scott, R. (2006). The aesthetic faculty. In Turner, M. (Ed.) *The artful mind: Cognitive science and the riddle of human creativity* (pp. 211–224). New York, NY: Oxford University Press.

Shapin, S. (2018). The scientific revolution. (2nd ed.) Chicago & London: University of Chicago Press.

Shipman, P. (2015). *The invaders. How humans and their dogs drove Neanderthals to extinction.* Cambridge, MA: Harvard University Press.

Shklar, J. (1989). The liberalism of fear. In Rosenblum, N.L. (Ed.), *Liberalism and the moral life* (pp. 21–38). Cambridge, MA: Harvard University Press.

Siviy, S. M. (1998). Neurobiological substrates of play behavior: glimpses into the structure and function of mammalian playfulness. In Beckoff, M. and Byers, J. (Eds.), *Animal play: Evolutionary, comparative, and ecological perspectives* (pp. 221–242). Cambridge, UK: Cambridge University Press.

Siviy, S. M. (2016). A brain motivated to play: insights into the neurobiology of playfulness. *Behaviour, 153* (6–7), 819–844.

Siviy, S. M., & Harrison, K. A. (2008). Effects of neonatal handling on play behavior and fear towards a predator odor in juvenile rats (Rattus norvegicus). *Journal of Comparative Psychology, 122*(1), 1–8.

Slade, A. (2014). Imagining fear: Attachment, threat and psychic experience. *Psychoanalytic Dialogues*, 24:253–266: Taylor & Francis Group, LLC.

Solnit, R. (2016). *Hope in the dark: Untold histories, wild possibilities.* Chicago, Illinois: Haymarket Books.

Spitz, E. H. (1988). The artistic image and the inward gaze: toward a merging of perspectives. *Psychoanalytic Review*, 75 (1), 111–128.

Spitz, E. H. (1996). Between image and child: Further reflections on picture books. *American Imago, 53*(2), 177–190.

Steen, F. (2006). The aesthetic faculty. In Turner, M. (Ed.) *The artful mind: Cognitive science and the riddle of human creativity* (pp. 57–72). New York, NY: Oxford University Press.

Stevens, J. R., & Hauser, M. D. (2005). Cooperative brains: Psychological constraints on the evolution of altruism. In Dehaene, S., Duhamel, J., Hauser, M., and Rizzolatti, G. (Eds.), *From monkey brain to human brain: A Fyssen Foundation symposium,* (pp. 159–187). Cambridge, MA: The MIT Press.

Stiglitz, J. (2009). Progress, what progress? *OECD Observer, 272.*

Strachey, J. (1959). Introduction. In Freud S., *The standard edition of the complete psychological works of Sigmund Freud, Volume XX (1925–1926): An autobiographical study, inhibitions, symptoms and anxiety, the question of lay analysis and other works* (pp. 75–176). London: The Hogarth Press.

Suddendorf, T. (2013). *The Gap: The science of what separates us from other animals.* New York, NY: Basic Books.

Suddendorf, T. (2013). Mental time travel: continuities and discontinuities. *Trends in cognitive sciences,* 17(4), 151–152.

Suler, J. (1996). Mental imagery in the organization and transformation of the self. Psychoanalytic Review, 83(5), 657–672.

Summers, F. (2000). The analyst's vision of the patient and therapeutic action. *Psychoanalytic Psychology,* 17(3), 547–564.

Takahashi, L. K., Nakashima, B. R., Hong, H., & Watanabe, K. (2005). The smell of danger: a behavioral and neural analysis of predator odor-induced fear. *Neuroscience & Biobehavioral Reviews,* 29(8), 1157–1167.

Tillich, P. (2000). *The courage to be* (2nd ed.). New Haven & London: Yale University Press. (Original work published 1958.)

Torchia, N. J. (1988). Curiositas in the early philosophical writings of Saint Augustine. *Augustinian Studies,* 19, 111–119.

Tranel, D., Gullickson, G., Koch, M., & Adolphs, R. (2006). Altered experience of emotion following bilateral amygdala damage. *Cognitive Neuropsychiatry,* 11(3), 219–232.

Turner, J.F. (2002). A brief history of illusion. *The International Journal of Psychoanalysis*, 83:1063–1082.

Turner, M. (2006). Prologue. In Turner, M. (Ed.) *The artful mind: Cognitive science and the riddle of human creativity* (pp. xv–xvi). New York, NY: Oxford University Press.

Turner, M. (2006). The aesthetic faculty. In Turner, M. (Ed.) *The artful mind: Cognitive science and the riddle of human creativity* (pp. 93–114). New York, NY: Oxford University Press.

Vaidyanathan, U., Hall, J. R., Patrick, C. J., & Bernat, E. M. (2011). Clarifying the role of defensive reactivity deficits in psychopathy and antisocial personality using startle reflex methodology. *Journal of Abnormal Psychology*, 120(1), 253–258.

Volchan, E., Souza, G. G., Franklin, C. M., Norte, C.E., Rocha-Rego, V., Oliveira, J., David, I. A., Mendlowicz, M.V., Freire Coutinho, E.S., Fiszman, A., Berger, W., Marques-Portella, C., & Figueria, I. (2011). Is there tonic immobility in humans? Biological evidence from victims of traumatic stress. *Biological Psychology* 88(1), 13–19.

Wardak, C., Ben Hamed, S., & Duhamel, J. R. (2005). Parietal mechanism of selective attention in monkeys and humans. In Dehaene, S., Duhamel, J., Hauser, M., and Rizzolatti, G. (Eds.), *From monkey brain to human rain: A Fyssen Foundation symposium*, (pp. 273–291). Cambridge, MA: The MIT Press.

Watts, A. (2011). *The wisdom of insecurity: A message for an age of anxiety.* (2nd ed.) New York, NY: Vintage Books. (Original work published 1951.)

Weinberg, E. (2006). Mentalization, affect regulation, and development of the self. *Journal of the American Psychoanalytic Association,* 54(1), 251–269.

Wertheim, J. (2010). Lost in space: the spiritual crisis of Newtonian cosmology. In Bryson, B. (Ed.), *Seeing further: The story of science, discovery, and the genius of the Royal Society.* (pp. 59–81). New York, NY: William Morrow / HarperCollins.

Whalen, P. J., Rauch, S. L., Etcoff, N. L., McInerney, S. C., Lee, M. B., & Jenike, M. A. (1998). Masked presentations of emotional facial expressions modulate amygdala activity without explicit knowledge. The Journal of Neuroscience, 18(1), 411–418.

Wilson, P. J. (1988). *The domestication of the human species*. New Haven and London: Yale University Press.

Wright, Kenneth (2009). Mirroring and attunement: *Self-realization in psychoanalysis and art*. London and New York: Routledge.

Zeki, S. (2006). The aesthetic faculty. In Turner, M. (Ed.) *The artful mind: Cognitive science and the riddle of human creativity* (pp. 243–270). New York, NY: Oxford University Press.

Zilles, K. (2005). Evolution of the human brain and comparative cyto- and receptor architecture. In Dehaene, S., Duhamel, J., Hauser, M., and Rizzolatti, G. (Eds.), *From monkey brain to human brain: A Fyssen Foundation symposium*, (pp. 41–56). Cambridge, MA: The MIT Press.

Endnotes

Introduction

1   See Tillich, P. (2000). *The courage to be* (2nd ed.). New Haven & London: Yale University Press. (Original work published 1958) See also Watts, A. (2011). *The wisdom of insecurity: A message for an age of anxiety.* (2nd ed.) New York, NY: Vintage Books. (Original work published 1951)

2   Bandelow, B., & Michaelis, S. (2015). Epidemiology of anxiety disorders in the 21st century. *Dialogues in clinical neuroscience*, 17(3), 327–335.

3   All patient material in this book is comprehensively disguised. In support of this, all relevant data, conclusions and meanings presented through these patient studies are a composite of clinical understandings from numerous patient cases demonstrating the salient variables. All of these efforts are to insure confidentiality, reliability and validity.

4   See Danforth, L. M. (1989). *Firewalking and religious healing: the Anastenaria of Greece and the American firewalking movement.* Princeton, NJ: Princeton University Press.

5   Ralph Waldo Emerson "Old Age," *Society and Solitude* (1870), p. 24

Chapter One

6   See Freud, S. (1900). The Interpretation of Dreams. The Standard Edition of the Complete Psychological Works of Sigmund Freud, Volume IV (1900):
See also Jung, C. G. (1917). On the psychology of the unconscious. *Coll. wks*, 7, 9–119.

7   Pinker, Steven (2008) The stuff of thought. New York: Penguin. p. 242–243

8   See Spitz, Rene A. "Hospitalism: An inquiry into the genesis of psychiatric conditions in early childhood." *The psychoanalytic study of the child* 1, no. 1 (1945): 53–74.

9   In using the term maternal, I am referring less to gender and more to a specific quality of loving care.

10 See Grotstein, J. S. (1993). A reappraisal of WRD Fairbairn. *Bulletin of the Menninger Clinic,* 57(4), 421.

11 See Burghardt, G. M. (1998). The evolutionary origins of play revisited: lessons from turtles. In Beckoff, M. and Byers, J. (Eds.), *Animal play: Evolutionary, comparative, and ecological perspectives* (pp. 1–26). Cambridge, UK: Cambridge University Press.

12 See Winnicott, D. W. (2012). *Playing and reality.* Routledge.

13 See Brown, S. (1998). Play as an organizing principle: clinical evidence and personal observations. In Beckoff, M. and Byers, J. (Eds.), *Animal Play: Evolutionary, Comparative, and Ecological Perspectives* (pp. 243–259). Cambridge, UK: Cambridge University Press.

14 See Goodall, J. (1977). Infant killing and cannibalism in free-living chimpanzees. Folia primatologica, 28(4), 259–282.

15 Sandseter, E. B. H. (2009). Children's expressions of exhilaration and fear in risky play. *Contemporary Issues in Early Childhood,* 10(2), 92–106.

16 See Cook, S., Peterson, L., & DiLillo, D. (2000). Fear and exhilaration in response to risk: An extension of a model of injury risk in a real-world context. *Behavior Therapy,* 30(1), 5–15.

17 Ibid.

18 Siegel, D.J. (2015) Brainstorm: The power and purpose of the teenage brain. Chicago. Penguin.

19 See Sandseter, E. B. H. (2009). Children's expressions of exhilaration and fear in risky play. *Contemporary Issues in Early Childhood,* 10(2), 92–106.

20 See Biben, M. (1998). Squirrel monkey playfighting: making the case for a cognitive training function for play. In Beckoff, M. and Byers, J. (Eds.), *Animal Play: Evolutionary, Comparative, and Ecological Perspectives* (pp. 161–182). Cambridge, UK: Cambridge University Press.

21 See Siviy, S. M., & Harrison, K. A. (2008). Effects of neonatal handling on play behavior and fear toward a predator odor in juvenile rats (Rattus norvegicus). *Journal of Comparative Psychology,* 122(1), 1–8.

22 See Mason, G.J., & Latham N.R. (2004). *Can't stop, won't stop: is stereotypy a reliable animal welfare indicator?* Abstract (13: pp. S57–69) from Universities Federation for Animal Welfare, The Old School, Brewhouse Hill, Wheathampstead, Hertfordshire, AL4 8AN, UK.

23   Ibid.

24   See Grassian, S. (2006). Psychiatric effects of solitary confinement. *Wash. UJL & Pol'y*, 22, 325.

Chapter Two

25   Ghent, E. (1990). Masochism, submission, surrender: Masochism as a perversion of surrender. *Contemporary psychoanalysis*, 26(1), 108–136.

26   See Tranel, D., Gullickson, G., Koch, M., & Adolphs, R. (2006). Altered experience of emotion following bilateral amygdala damage. *Cognitive Neuropsychiatry*, 11(3), 219–232.
     See also, Feinstein, J. S., Adolphs, R., Damasio, A., & Tranel, D. (2011). The human amygdala and the induction and experience of fear. *Current Biology*, 21(1), 34–38.

27   See LeDoux, J. E., Cicchetti, P., Xagoraris, A., & Romanski, L. M. (1990). The lateral amygdaloid nucleus: sensory interface of the amygdala in fear conditioning. *Journal of Neuroscience*, 10(4), 1062–1069.

28   See Adolphs, R. (2013). The biology of fear. *Current Biology*, 23(2), R79–R93.

29   See LeDoux, J. E., Cicchetti, P., Xagoraris, A., & Romanski, L. M. (1990). The lateral amygdaloid nucleus: sensory interface of the amygdala in fear conditioning. Journal of Neuroscience, 10(4), 1062–1069.

30   See Panksepp, J. & Biven, L. (2012). *The archeology of mind: Neuroevolutionary origins of human emotions.* New York: Norton & Company.

31   Amis, M. (1996) The Information. London: Vintage.

32   See Frijda, N. H. (1987). Emotion, cognitive structure, and action tendency. *Cognition and emotion*, 1(2), 115–143.

33   See Panksepp, J. & Biven, L. (2012). *The archeology of mind: Neuroevolutionary origins of human emotions.* New York: Norton & Company.

34   Watts, A. (2011). *The wisdom of insecurity: A message for an age of anxiety.* (2nd ed.) New York, NY: Vintage Books. (Original work published 1951)

35   See Corrigan, F.M. (2014). Defense responses: Frozen, suppressed, truncated, obstructed, and malfunctioning. In Lanius, U. F., Paulsen, S. L., & Corrigan, F. M. (Eds.), *Neurobiology and treatment of traumatic dissociation: Towards an embodied self.* (Kindle edition. pp. 131–152). New

York, NY: Springer Publishing Company.

Chapter Three

36   Aristotle, *The Art of Rhetoric,* 153

37   See Muris, P., Merckelbach, H., & Collaris, R. (1997). Common childhood fears and their origins. *Behaviour research and therapy,* 35(10), 929–937.

38   See Hall, G. S. (1907). *Youth: Its education, regimen, and hygiene.* Comet Content Providers.

39   See Suddendorf, T. (2013). *The Gap: The science of what separates us from other animals.* New York, NY: Basic Books.
      See also Shipman, P. (2015). *The invaders. How humans and their dogs drove Neanderthals to extinction.* Cambridge, MA: Harvard University Press.

40   See Antunes A, Troyer JL, Roelke ME, Pecon-Slattery J, Packer C, et al, 2008

41   See Schaller, M., Park, J. H., & Mueller, A. (2003). Fear of the dark: Interactive effects of beliefs about danger and ambient darkness on ethnic stereotypes. *Personality and Social Psychology Bulletin,* 29(5), 637–649.

42   Schaller, M., Park, J. H., & Mueller, A. (2003). Fear of the dark: Interactive effects of beliefs about danger and ambient darkness on ethnic stereotypes. *Personality and Social Psychology Bulletin* p. 637

43   See Turner, M. (2006). Prologue. In Turner, M. (Ed.) *The artful mind: Cognitive science and the riddle of human creativity* (pp. xv-xvi). New York, NY: Oxford University Press.

44   See Hublin, J. J. (2005). Evolution of the human brain and comparative paleoanthropology. In Dehaene, S., Hauser, M. D., Duhamel, J. R., & Rizzolatti, G. (Eds.), *From monkey brain to human brain: A Fyssen Foundation symposium* (pp. 57–71). Cambridge, MA: The MIT Press.
See also Wilson, P. J. (1988). *The domestication of the human species.* New Haven and London: Yale University Press.

45   See Hublin, J. J. (2005). Evolution of the human brain and comparative paleoanthropology. In Dehaene, S., Hauser, M. D., Duhamel, J. R., & Rizzolatti, G. (Eds.), From monkey brain to human brain: A Fyssen Foundation symposium (pp. 57–71). Cambridge, MA: The MIT Press.

46   See Binsted, G., Brownell, K., Vorontsova, Z., Heath, M., & Saucier, D. (July 31, 2007). Visuomotor system uses target features unavailable to conscious awareness. *Proceedings of the National Academy of Sciences*, 104(31), 12669–12672.

47   See Schaller, M. (2014, Oct). When and how disgust is and is not implicated in the behavioral immune system. Evolutionary Behavioral Sciences, 8(4) pp. 251–256.

48   See Leslie, A.M. & Frith, U. (1988). Autistic children's understanding of seeing, knowing and believing. *British Journal of Developmental Psychology*, 6(4), 315–324, The British Psychological Society.

49   Lakoff, G., & Johnson, M. (2008). Metaphors we live by. University of Chicago press.

50   Pinker, S. (2007). The stuff of thought: Language as a window into human nature. Penguin. pp. 242–243.

51   See Humphrey, N. (2002). *The inner eye.* Oxford University Press on Demand. p. 76.

Chapter Four

52   See Barlow, D. H. (2002). *Anxiety and its disorders: The nature and treatment of anxiety and panic* (2nd ed.). New York, NY: Guilford press.

53   See Panksepp, J. & Biven, L. (2012). *The archeology of mind: Neuroevolutionary origins of human emotions.* New York: Norton & Company.

54   See Ngui, P. W. (1969). Koro epidemic in Singapore. *Australian and New Zealand Journal of Psychiatry*, 3(3), 263–266.

55   See Barlow, D. H. (2002). *Anxiety and its disorders: The nature and treatment of anxiety and panic* (2nd ed.). New York, NY: Guilford press.

56   See Yerkes, R. M. & Dodson, J. D. (1908). The relationship of strength of stimulus to rapidity of habit formation. *Journal of Comparative Neurology and Psychology, 18,* 459–482.

57   See Liddell, H. S. (1949). Adaptation on the threshold of intelligence.

58   See Barlow, D. H. (2002). *Anxiety and its disorders: The nature and treatment of anxiety and panic.* (2nd ed.) New York, NY: Guilford press. P. 9

59   See Suddendorf, T. (2013). Mental time travel: continuities and discontinuities. Trends in cognitive sciences, 17(4), 151–152. Chicago.

60   See Sibrava, N. J., & Borkovec, T. D. (2006). The cognitive avoidance theory of worry. *Worry and its psychological disorders: Theory, assessment*

and treatment, 239–256.

61 See Crouch, T. A., Lewis, J. A., Erickson, T. M., & Newman, M. G. (2017). Prospective investigation of the contrast avoidance model of generalized anxiety and worry. *Behavior therapy,* 48(4), 544–556.

62 See Sibrava, N. J., & Borkovec, T. D. (2006). The cognitive avoidance theory of worry. *Worry and its psychological disorders: Theory, assessment and treatment,* 239–256.

63 See Ellenberger, H. F. (1970). *The discovery of the unconscious: The history and evolution of dynamic psychiatry* (Vol. 1, pp. 280–281). New York: Basic Books.

64 See Freud, S., & Breuer, J. (2004). *Studies in hysteria.* Penguin.

65 See Faranda, F. The purposive self and the dreaming mind. (2003) Dissertation.

66 See Jung, C. (1963) Memories, dreams, reflections. New York: Pantheon Books.

67 See Freud, S., Jung, C. G., & McGlashan, A. (1994). The Freud-Jung Letters: *The Correspondence Between Sigmund Freud and CG Jung* (Vol. 135). Princeton University Press.

68 Reiff, Phillip (1979) Freud: The Mind of the Moralist. The University of Chicago Press.

69 Faranda, Frank (2003). The Purposive Self and the Dreaming Mind. Dissertation, Adelphi University.

70 Loewenstein, S. F. (1985). Freud's metapsychology revisited. *Social Casework,* 66(3), 139–151.

71 *The Illusion of Conscious Will,* Daniel M. Wegner.

72 Donald, M. (2001). *A mind so rare: The evolution of human consciousness.* New York / London: W.W. Norton & Co. p.3

73 Donald, M. (2001). *A mind so rare: The evolution of human consciousness.* New York / London: W.W. Norton & Co. p. 28

74 Minsky, M. The society of mind. (1988). New York: Simon and Scheuster. p.306

75 Libet, B. (1985). Unconscious cerebral initiative and the role of conscious will in voluntary action. The Behavioral and Brain Sciences 8: 529–566.

Chapter Six

76   See Damasio, A.R. Self Comes to Mind. New York, NY: Random House.

77   Andreasen, N. *The Creating Brain: The Neuroscience of Genius*, p. 62–63.

78   See Kosslyn, S. M. (2005). Reflective thinking and mental imagery: A perspective on the development of posttraumatic stress disorder. *Development and Psychopathology*, 17(3), 851–863.

79   See Fauconnier, G. (2001). Conceptual blending and analogy. In Gentner, D., Holyoak, K., & Kokinov, B. (Eds.), *The analogical mind: Perspectives from cognitive science*, (pp. 255–286). Cambridge, MA: The MIT Press.

80   See Donald, M. (2001). *A mind so rare: The evolution of human consciousness*. New York / London: W.W. Norton & Co.

81   Rattansi, P. (1988). Newton and the wisdom of the ancients. In Fauvel, J., Flood, R., Shortland, M. & Wilson, R. (Eds.), *Let Newton be!* (pp. 185–201). Oxford, England: Oxford University Press p. 185.

82   Augustine, Confessions Book X para 54

83   ibid, para 53

84   ibid, para 56

85   Torchia, N. J. (1988). Curiositas in the early philosophical writings of Saint Augustine. *Augustinian Studies*, 19, p. 112

86   Harrison, P. (2001). Curiosity, forbidden knowledge, and the reformation of natural philosophy in early modern England. Isis, 92(2), 265–290. p. 267–268.

87   See Moller, V. (2019). *The map of knowledge. A thousand-year history of how classical ideas were lost and found*. New York, NY: Doubleday.

88   See Harrison, P. (2001). Curiosity, forbidden knowledge, and the reformation of natural philosophy in early modern England. *Isis*, 92(2), 265–290.

89   Going forward I will use the term "mother" in a non-gendered way to refer to the primary caregiver.

90   Hublin, J. J. (2005). Evolution of the human brain and comparative paleoanthropology. In Dehaene, S., Hauser, M. D., Duhamel, J. R., & Rizzolatti, G. (Eds.), *From monkey brain to human brain: A Fyssen Foundation symposium* (pp. 57–71). Cambridge, MA: The MIT Press.

91   Hublin, J. J. (2005). Evolution of the human brain and comparative paleoanthropology. In Dehaene, S., Hauser, M. D., Duhamel, J. R., & Rizzolatti, G. (Eds.), *From monkey brain to human brain: A Fyssen Foundation symposium* (pp. 57–71). Cambridge, MA: The MIT.

92   Slade, A. (2014). Imagining fear: Attachment, threat and psychic experience. *Psychoanalytic Dialogues*, 24: 253–266: Taylor & Francis Group, LLC.

93   See Gibson, E. J., & Walk, R. D. (1960). "The visual cliff." *Scientific American*, 202(4), 64–71.

94   See Klinnert, M. D., Campos, J., Source, J. F., Emde, R. N., & Svejda, M. J. (1983). Social referencing. *Emotion*, 2, 57–86.

Chapter Seven

95   D.W. Winnicott (1971) p. xx.

96   Dan Siegel Prunning.

97   Rushkoff, D. (2019) Team Human. New York, NY: Norton.

98   See Levack, B. P. (2006). *The witch-hunt in early modern europe*, (3rd ed.). Great Britain: Pearson Education Limited.

99   See Gleick, J. (2010). At the beginning: more things in heaven and earth. In Bryson, B. (Ed.), *Seeing further: The story of science, discovery, and the genius of the Royal Society*. (pp. 17–35). New York, NY: William Morrow / HarperCollins.

100 See Dolnick, E. (2011). *The clockwork universe: Isaac Newton, the Royal Society, and the birth of the modern world*. New York: Harper Collins.

101 See The Diary of Samuel Pepys.

102 See Gleick, J. (2010). At the beginning: more things in heaven and earth. In Bryson, B. (Ed.), *Seeing further: The story of science, discovery, and the genius of the Royal Society*. (pp. 17–35). New York, NY: William Morrow / HarperCollins.

103 See BUTTERFIELD, H. (1957). *The origins of modern science 1300–1800* (2nd ed.). London: G. Bell and Sons Ltd.

104 See Gleick, J. (2010). At the beginning: more things in heaven and earth. In Bryson, B. (Ed.), *Seeing further: The story of science, discovery, and the genius of the Royal Society*. (pp. 17–35). New York, NY: William Morrow / HarperCollins.

105 From the diary of Pepys in Gleick, J. (2010). At the beginning: more things in heaven and earth. In Bryson, B. (Ed.), *Seeing further: The story of science, discovery, and the genius of the Royal Society.* (pp. 17–35). New York, NY: William Morrow / HarperCollins. P. 29

106 Bacon, Francis, (1620). *Novum Organum.* In Hutchins, R. M. (Ed.).(1952). *Great books of the western world: Francis Bacon* (Vol. 30, pp. 107–195). Chicago, Ill.: W. Benton / Encyclopedia Britannica p. 135

107 See Harrison, P. (2001). Curiosity, forbidden knowledge, and the reformation of natural philosophy in early modern England. Isis, 92(2), 265–290.

108 Quoted in Ball, P. (2010). Making stuff: from Bacon to Bakelit. In Bryson, B. (Ed.), *Seeing further: The story of science, discovery, and the genius of the Royal Society.* (pp. 295–319). New York, NY: William Morrow / HarperCollins. P. 299

109 Shapin, S. (2018). *The scientific revolution.* (2nd ed.) Chicago & London: University of Chicago Press. p. 20

110 Bacon, Francis, (1620). *Novum Organum.* In Hutchins, R. M. (Ed.).(1952). *Great books of the western world: Francis Bacon* (Vol. 30, pp. 107–195). Chicago, Ill.: W. Benton / Encyclopedia Britannica p. 110

111 See Fosshage, J.L. (2004). The Role of Empathy and Interpretation in the Therapeutic Process: Commentary on Discussions of Salee Jenkins's Clinical Case. Progress in Self Psychology, 20:325-334.

112 Bacon, Francis, (1620). Novum Organum. In Hutchins, R. M. (Ed.).(1952). *Great books of the western world: Francis Bacon* (Vol. 30, pp. 107–195). Chicago, Ill.: W. Benton / Encyclopedia Britannica. P. 110

113 Bacon quoted in Gleick, J. (2003). *Isaac Newton.* New York: Random House. P. 63

114 Bacon, Francis, (1627). New Atlantis. In Hutchins, R. M. (Ed.).(1952). *Great books of the western world: Francis Bacon* (Vol. 30, pp. 199–214). Chicago, Ill.: W. Benton / Encyclopedia Britannica. P. 207

Chapter Eight

115 Williamson, M.

116 Richtel, Matt. New York Times, 7 April 2019.

117 CDC. Antibiotic Resistance Threats in the United States, 2019. Atlan-

ta, GA: US Department of Health and Human Services, CDC; 2019.

118 The term spiritual bypass was coined by the Buddhist psychotherapist John Welwood in the 1980s. He conceptualized a state in which spiritual ideas are used to avoid psychological pain.

119 Kurzweil, R. (2005) The Singularity Is Near: When Humans Transcend Biology. New York: Penguin.

Chapter Nine

120 Glassner, B. (2010). *The Culture of Fear: Why Americans Are Afraid of the Wrong Things: Crime, Drugs, Minorities, Teen Moms, Killer Kids, Muta.* Hachette UK.

121 See Alleg, H. (2006). *The question* (J. Calder, Trans.). Lincoln, NE: U of Nebraska Press. (Original work published 1958).

122 See Sartre, J. (2006). Preface. In H. Alleg, *The question* (J. Calder, Trans.), (pp. xxvii-xliv). Lincoln, NE: U of Nebraska Press. (Original work published 1958).

123 Brown, B. (2012) *Daring Greatly. How the Courage to Be Vulnerable Transforms the Way We Live, Love, Parent, and Lead.* New York, NY: Avery.

Index

About the Author

Dr. Frank Faranda is a clinical psychologist in New York City with seventeen years of experience in private practice. He spends his days helping people deal with fear and imagination. He earned his master's degree in developmental psychology and education from Columbia University, Teacher's College, and his PhD in clinical psychology from the Derner Institute at Adelphi University. He was awarded postdoctoral fellowships from New York University's Postdoctoral Program in Psychotherapy and Psychoanalysis, and the Rusk Institute of Rehabilitation Medicine. Dr. Faranda has also taught several courses at the New School, including, "The Development of the Self" and "An Introduction to Jung." Over the last several years he has published academic articles on mind, metaphor, and imagination in preparation for this book, and has also guest-edited two themed journal issues for *Psychoanalytic Inquiry*.

Mango Publishing, established in 2014, publishes an eclectic list of books by diverse authors—both new and established voices—on topics ranging from business, personal growth, women's empowerment, LGBTQ studies, health, and spirituality to history, popular culture, time management, decluttering, lifestyle, mental wellness, aging, and sustainable living. We were recently named 2019's #1 fastest growing independent publisher by *Publishers Weekly*. Our success is driven by our main goal, which is to publish high quality books that will entertain readers as well as make a positive difference in their lives.

Our readers are our most important resource; we value your input, suggestions, and ideas. We'd love to hear from you—after all, we are publishing books for you!

Please stay in touch with us and follow us at:

Facebook: Mango Publishing

Twitter: @MangoPublishing

Instagram: @MangoPublishing

LinkedIn: Mango Publishing

Pinterest: Mango Publishing

Sign up for our newsletter at www.mangopublishinggroup.com and receive a free book!

Join us on Mango's journey to reinvent publishing, one book at a time.

CPSIA information can be obtained
at www.ICGtesting.com
Printed in the USA
BVHW031438300320
576346BV00001B/1

9 781642 500578